To Jeremy
Thank you so much!

PTSD

No Apologies

An Anthology From Lemon Press

WWW.PTSDNOAPOLOGIES.COM

© COPYRIGHTED 2015 BY LEMON PRESS
ALL RIGHTS RESERVED.
PRINTED IN THE UNITED STATES OF AMERICA.
ISBN- 978-1-936617-29-6

PUBLISHED BY LEMON PRESS
ACWORTH, GA

WWW.LEMONPRESSPUBLISHING.COM

This is an Anthology. All works are used with permission from the Author. All Contributors retain the Original Copyrights for their work.

Disclaimer: The views and opinions expressed in this book are those of the authors and do not necessarily reflect the official policy or position of Lemon Press Publishing or our Sponsors.

All rights reserved. In accordance with the U.S. Copyright Act of 1976, the scanning, uploading, and electronic sharing of any part of this book without the permission of the publisher constitute unlawful piracy and theft of the author's intellectual property. If you would like permission to use this author's material work other than for reviews, prior written permission must be obtained by contacting the publisher. Thank you for your support of the author's rights.

Lemon Press Publishing

PO BOX 459

Emerson, GA 30137

Honoring the Memory of

Navy Seal Danny Carson

To those that dwell in darkness.
Seek out the light.

~Lynn Hubbard

DEDICATION

This book is dedicated to all those suffering.
PTSD is real, and you are not alone.

Special thanks to my book advisors:
Cindy Smith & Tom "Knobby" Walsh.
Thank you for all of your hard work
and dedication to our Vets.

Let's save some.

Table of Contents

DEDICATION V
INTRODUCTION XI
BY LYNN HUBBARD XI
FOREWORD XV
BY CINDY SMITH XV
1 I WAS NOT THE ONLY ONE 1
RANGER BILL 1
2 BROKEN SOLDIERS – COMING HOME 8
POEM BY DWANE BARR 8
3 EVENTUALLY IT ALL FADES INTO NOTHINGNESS
GERALD "DINO" MCGRATH 10
4 ANDERSONVILLE 13
POEM BY LYNN HUBBARD 13
5 RURAL ROUTE 15
ART BY KERRY "DOC" PARDUE 15
6 KEEP YOUR BACK TO THE WALL 16
ANONYMOUS 16
7 ANDY BERRY, AMERICAN HERO 24
BY CHARLIE MAY 24
8 THE UNKNOWN SOLDIER 28
POEM BY LYNN HUBBARD 28
9 DANNY'S STORY 29
AS RECALLED BY AUTHOR JON BRODERICK 29
10 YOUR LIFE MADE A DIFFERENCE TO ME 39
POEM BY KERRY "DOC" PARDUE 39
11 INVISIBLE 43
ANONYMOUS 43
12 FREEDOM'S LIGHT 50

SONG BY CHARLIE MAY 50
13 I AM NO STRANGER TO PTSD 53
RON ASBY 53
14 INVISIBLE SCARS 58
POEM BY LYNN HUBBARD 58
15 I EXIST TO LIVE 60
HUGH LEE YOUNG 60
16 NO MORE 69
ART BY BARTHOLOMEW GRAY 69
17 DON'T LET IT GET THE BETTER OF YOU 70
DAVID SILFER 70
18 THE DREAM 78
POEM BY PADEN SMITH 78
19 IN AN INSTANT 81
JOHN FREDERICKS 81
20 LIVING WITH A STRANGER 102
REBECCA FREDRICKS 102
21 VIEW OF AN ARMY TRUCK DRIVER 105
JAMES (JIM) FILHART 105
22 THE THINGS THEY CARRY 109
ART BY CHRIS DEROUX 109
23 THIS STUFF ONLY HAPPENS TO THE LIVING ... 110
RON PAPALEONI, USN CPO RETIRED 110
24 PATRIOT GUARD RIDERS 117
SONG BY CINDY SMITH AND T. B. BURTON 117
25 MY OWN LITTLE WAR 120
KENNESAW TAYLOR 120
26 THE LAST BREATH 128
ART BY BERNIE "DOC" DUFF 128
27 FIRE - FIRE - FIRE - ON THE FLIGHT DECK AFT 129

THOMAS H. YARMOSH 129
AS TOLD TO CINDY SMITH 129
28 OLD MEN WITH BROKEN HEARTS 136
SONG BY CHARLIE MAY 136
29 LIFE HASN'T ALWAYS BEEN EASY. 138
ANONYMOUS 138
30 ANOTHER PTSD NIGHT 142
POEM BY KERRY "DOC" PARDUE 142
31 THE MANY FACES OF PTSD 143
GEORGE WOODRUFF 143
32 THOSE WHO CAME HOME 153
DWANE BARR 153
33 MY JOURNEY HOME 155
ZACH CHOATE 155
34 EVERY DAY IS MEMORIAL DAY 163
POEM BY KERRY "DOC" PARDUE 163
35 THE LONG DARK ROAD 165
JIM ELLIOTT 165
YOUR STORY 187
SPONSORS 199
CONTRIBUTORS INFORMATION: 201
INDEX 203

x

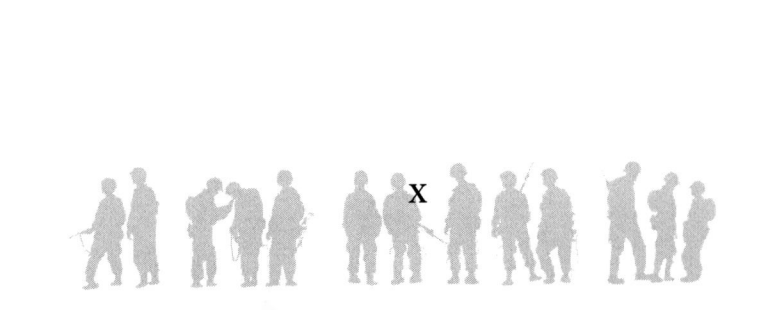

INTRODUCTION

By Lynn Hubbard

Some memories stay with us forever. I used to live in New Jersey. There wasn't much self-sacrifice at our school. Then one day in junior high we had a guest speaker. The entire school was herded into the auditorium to hear him talk. There was much chatter and mayhem as we fumbled for seats next to our friends. Once more or less settled, the Principal introduced us to a man.

He was different from the typical stiff tied puppet that was usually announced. This guy was not perfect, he had scars. This fact in itself caught our attention.

Then he began to speak, and we listened to his story.

He had been injured in Vietnam. He was on a patrol boat on a river. The air was thick with smog and the river was even filthier. He stood on deck keeping watch, an enemy boat approached and fighting commenced. A phosphorus grenade exploded in his hand and ignited him. He was thrown free from the vessel, and into the oil filled river. The river burned and so did he.

He ducked under the water to escape the flames, but the water was so polluted they would not extinguish. He started to sink, yet the fire still burned. He burned all the way down, and all the way back up as he swam for the surface.

Even then he had a zest for life. It would have been easy to just give in and be engulfed. But he wasn't done yet.

Guided by the flames above, he broke through gasping for air. He was pulled back onto the boat and the flames were beat out.

I can't imagine the agonizing pain he must have went through just to live. But live he did. He recuperated, slowly. And fate brought him to my school.

By now the room was silent. Each lost in their own thoughts. And then he started to yell. To yell about how we are wasting our lives.

Lives that we have, due to the sacrifices of our soldiers.

It was at this point in time that the staff started to evacuate us from the room. They escorted us out and I could still hear him shouting out his message.

For us to Live.

That we have a purpose.

And then we were rushed down the hallways, and back to our safe little rooms.

Then it happened.

The teacher apologized to us.

FOR HIM.

I was pissed then, and I'm still pissed now.

So this book is being written for him. And for anyone who needs to be reminded that they have a purpose. That they need to live.

Living is so much more than just surviving. Surviving is the easy part. Living is hard, but oh so worth the effort.

No Apologies.

FOREWORD

By Cindy Smith

PTSD is a touchy subject. My assignment was to collect stories on how men and women were dealing with their PTSD on a personal basis. All for the benefit of others, who are diagnosed with PTSD, to read and know they are not alone. During this book pilgrimage, I'm afraid I may have offended a few folks with the mere mention of the word. What I discovered was that for every ten people who had nothing to say, I eventually found one or two that did.

I can't tell you what an honor it has been to listen to the contributors and help them write their story! They reminisced like it was yesterday, recalling intimate details as they spoke. Sometimes painful, sometimes difficult. Other times during the interviews, I saw a sparkle in their eye, or heard a chuckle in their voice. It was like they had made a mental decision in their mind that no matter what, *they preserved and are now happy in their lives.*

PTSD is everywhere. *Post-Traumatic Stress Disorder* is a mental health condition. According to an online description, it occurs after a person experiences a 'traumatic' event, such as an assault, warfare, serious injury or terrifying occurrence. Before we gave it a name, PTSD for soldiers was referred to as 'shell-shock' or 'battle fatigue'. Symptoms can include anything from disturbing flashbacks to recurrent nightmares, and affect the functioning of everyday life. Camo-wearing soldiers are not the only ones afflicted with PTSD. It is an equal opportunity condition that goes beyond the battlefield and nudges itself into the lives of Police Officers and Public Servants, victims of serious crimes and people who suffered traumatic situations in their lives, just to name a few. Although doctors may prescribe medications to treat PTSD, they can only treat the SYMPTOMS.

Lynn Hubbard, owner of Lemon Press Publishing, had an idea that would offer people a chance to share what they've been through with their own personal PTSD, in an effort to help others. The result is this book, a compilation of stories by men and women, expressed in their own views, raw, unfiltered and frankly 'no hold barred.' Their words offer hope and encouragement to not only the reader, but conducts as a form of therapy to the writer as well.

We civilians live in a rose colored world, a bubble, safe from the war zones that our soldiers see on a daily basis. The only way for us to have an inkling of an idea of what a soldier goes through on a tour of duty is by reading a book or watching a Hollywood movie. How can we fully understand something we do not feel? Perhaps by reading the stories, we can get a glimpse inside the anatomy of PTSD.

When telling me his story, one man explained it like this - PTSD is not something you can generally see with your eyes. Some soldiers come home with lost limbs or scars, and you immediately know what's wrong with them. You feel for their loss, you grieve for their misfortune. But, when you have PTSD, an invisible condition, you feel embarrassed and guilty because your body is whole. You want to block it out, hide it and pretend it doesn't exist, or deny the fact that you have it.

While Lynn and I were preparing our thoughts about the book, we asked to meet with Patriot Guard Riders members, Ron "Pappy" Papaleoni and Tom Walsh, for their input. At the meeting, I was quoting the statistics I had gathered from government websites pertaining to PTSD. According to the Department of Veteran Affairs, over 100,000 vets are homeless and living on the streets and almost half of them are diagnosed with PTSD. According to the PTSD Foundation of America, 1 in every 3 U.S. Soldiers returning home today are diagnosed with PTSD. *"Under estimated,"* Pappy told me, shaking his head. *"Everyone is effected one way or another when they serve. Everyone."* And, he is right.

Trying to put a number on veterans with PTSD is like trying to count the stars on a clear summer night. There are just so many, and sooner or later, you just get lost in the count. Suicides are increasing every day at an alarming rate. The lack of understanding, insufficient treatments, along with misidentification of PTSD are all contributing factors.

When I was a teenager in high school, I bought a POW/MIA metal bracelet for $3.00. The concept was to wear the bracelet until the soldier, whose name was engraved on it, returned home. I had a math teacher who spent the entire hour of class discussing the war in Vietnam. I remember the protests and war scenes on TV, and although there were plenty of things I didn't understand, there wasn't a day that went by that I didn't think about those boys over there. Some from families I knew personally. I did the only thing I knew to do to show I cared - I wore the bracelet.

That is why I accepted the assignment from Lynn to help with the writing of this book. It gave me the opportunity to get involved again and actually *do something to make a difference.* The men I interviewed will always remain close to my heart. God bless them all.

I go back to thinking about those scenes on television in the early '70's, the protestors in opposition to the war in Vietnam. "Draft beer, not boys" and "Hey, hey, LBJ, how many kids did you kill today?" It made me angry. I would stare at the bracelet on my wrist and wonder how 'my' soldier was feeling at that very minute. If he was safe. If he was alive. I pondered what it was going to be like for him when (and if) he returned home.

My son, Paden, enlisted in the Army during his 11th grade of high school. I was so proud of him. That summer, he and his friend, Brandon, left for basic training in South Carolina. They were young boys, barely had turned seventeen years old. When they returned home from training, they proudly wore their Army fatigues to the local mall *(admittedly with the intent of impressing the opposite sex!)* What they encountered was not what they expected. An elderly, well-dressed woman approached them. She voiced her displeasure and wrath of seeing the young soldiers in uniform by spitting on them and calling them names. Paden told me later, that he and Brandon stood there, wiped the spit off and told the woman, "Ma'am, it's because of Soldiers like us, you have the *freedom* of speech to say what you just said."

Our Country stands strong because our men and women fought and died for the freedom we have today. It only takes a second, to greet a veteran or soldier, and tell him how much you appreciate his service. No, a simple acknowledgment won't prevent PTSD, or cure PTSD, but a little courtesy goes a long way. Remembrance is something we cannot allow to go out of style, lest their sacrifices were in vain.

PTSD is not going away. It won't disappear just because no one wants to talk about it. Apparently, (from the stories I've been told) the treatment and 'pills' can only do so much. Each person has to find their own individual way to confront their emotions and stress, to adapt and overcome. This book is only the beginning.

The goal of Lynn Hubbard and Lemon Press Publishing is to donate a copy of NO APOLOGIES to every VA hospital in the United States. It will be funded by public sales, with proceeds used for the hospital distributions.

Everyone has a story. Maybe now is the time to write yours. You don't have to be a prolific writer, and if you prefer, you don't have to write at all. We will write it for you. If you've been diagnosed with PTSD, or believe you have it, we've left several blank pages at the end of this book. When you feel like writing your thoughts, fill in the pages. We will be collecting more PTSD stories for future volumes. Contact Lemon Press Publishing to submit yours. There is always someone out there that needs to hear what YOU have to say.

Cindy is the author of several books (Time in Contention, A Cowgirl's Taste for Life, Cowboy World children's series) and a Country/Western Singer/Songwriter. She's a member of the Western Music Association, The Atlanta Country Music Hall of Fame, The Georgia Country and Gospel Music Association, the Single Action Shooting Society and the Patriot Guard Riders.

1

I WAS NOT THE ONLY ONE

Ranger Bill

Like many other individuals who have experienced and are suffering from what is now called PTSD, I denied having a problem while watching my life fall apart around me. I spent years of my life watching things go sour not realizing that I was constantly undermining or deliberately sabotaging whatever I did. Every time things would go right for me I would do something to screw it up.

I am truly blessed to be one of the lucky ones who have been able to overcome my life of fear, always being on the defense and ready to either fight or run away, and those horrible, horrible day dreams and nightmares. In the beginning, for an almost 15 year period, I would have intervals of maintaining an almost normal existence. But, it would seem like out of nowhere, I would once again start to do things that would hurt whatever I was trying to accomplish. I did not really start to get a handle on it until sometime in 1981.

I had been drinking really heavily for days when my wife, Lynn, and I got into an argument concerning my perpetually drunken state. She had finally reached her limit and took the kids and left me going to stay with a friend. She had often threatened to do this but had never really gotten up and walked out the door before. Later that evening, and after another bottle of bourbon, I became severely depressed. Lynn had been the one good thing in my life that gave me any hope of finding true happiness in my existence and I had now lost her forever.

For the first time in my life I sat and wrote a suicide note meaning with full intent on following through. I sat for a long, long time after completing it, re-reading the note over and over. I then loaded my 12 gauge shotgun and took off my right boot and sock to insert my big toe into the trigger guard and sat down in my kitchen chair and prepared to end all of my misery right there.

All of a sudden a picture flashed in my mind of Lynn and my children walking in and seeing the mess that used to be me. I could not hurt them in that manner. I then sat there and tried to think of where I would go to end my worthless good for nothing life.

Only one name came to mind. A friend who I had worked with on a previous job, a fellow Veteran who although also drank to excess, had it together much more than I did and would understand.

Shotgun on safe and boot back on, I was out the door. Arriving at "Joe's" house with a fresh bottle of bourbon, I told him of my plans. He did not try to talk me out of what I wanted to do but insisted that we drink the fresh bottle first. I knew I could trust this Brother. We agreed that we would drink up and then I would go out into his woodshed and do the deed. Somehow sitting with him and drinking, he got me to talking, and I think I poured out my heart and soul to him.

He looked at me and asked me why I had to

hate myself so much. He pointed out that Hell yes I had done some absolutely terrible things in my life but most of them were done in the name of survival and besides, I wasn't the only one. He then looked me in the eye and told me that if I knew what he had done in his life, I would probably hate him.

He stared into my very essence and told me that I was not the only one. That everyone carried a burden that they were ashamed of. In that moment of time it was like God slapped me in the face. A light came on and for the first time I could see that the root of most of my problems was GUILT. I sat there on his living room couch and cried like a baby. I made the realization that Guilt had done more harm to my life than any other single thing.

Was I cured at that point? Absolutely not, but it was the start of me learning that first and foremost, I had to like myself before I could be a complete human being and fulfill my life's destiny.

Am I cured NOW? I would like to think so. I know that I have made tons of progress but every once in a while, thankfully not that often anymore, I will sit straight up in bed struggling to get away from one of "those" dreams. And, when I am sick my very first reaction is to pull back and hide, not wanting anyone to know that I might be vulnerable. And deep in my mind, every great once in a while, I will remember something that I truly wish had never occurred. But I know it did and there is absolutely nothing that I can do about it now except try to make amends to the universe by being the best possible person that I can be.

That doesn't mean being someone I'm not, but it means channeling my strengths and diminishing my faults into a lifestyle that allows me to feel good about myself at the end of each day. What has worked for me may not work for another. I have never received any professional help in this. As, I really do not trust Doctors. I think poorly of Mental Health Professionals as most of them that I have come in contact with in my life, have had visible problems of their own that was very obvious to me.

Please do not let my prejudices cause you not to seek professional help. I have known persons who swear that a Shrink or Counselor has helped them through a crisis. My intolerance is based on my life's experiences, mine and mine alone which has caused me to mistrust this profession. I truly believe that the most important thing is to not face it alone.

Talk with someone, be it a professional, a friend, fellow Veteran, or your spouse or lover. Someone you can trust. Why it took me so many years to face it was that I was ashamed to tell anybody how I was feeling for fear of being laughed at or viewed as some kind of mental case. Although my wife knew something was wrong, and often tried to get me to talk about it, I was afraid that she would lose all respect for me if she knew the truth.

Don't be dumb like me. After my breakthrough, I spent several days with my friend trying to wrap my head around what I had learned and sobering up. I then approached my wife, and for the first time in our relationship, was brutally honest on the reasons for my erratic behavior. Although severely angry and suspicious at first my wife heard me out and has always been there for me when my demons would surface, even to this day.

If you experience these feelings in today's world you often hear things like "I understand" or "you are not alone" and I know your inner voice is telling you "Bullshit".

The truth is nobody can truly understand how you personally feel inside, BUT, there are those that can understand enough to help you to help yourself. Please do not face this alone.

Good Luck Brother.

Live/Ride Proud.

Ranger Bill

2

BROKEN SOLDIERS — COMING HOME

Poem by Dwane Barr

Even with buddies he felt alone, Vietnam had become his new home. But with pride he saluted the flag that unfurled, the best known icon in the entire world.

Great love of country made him enlist; Family and friends were very missed. But it was a job that had to be done, when they asked for soldiers, he was glad to be one.

Down in the jungles everything green, the enemy was clever, and seldom seen. They walked miles in a day, trying to keep Charlie at bay.

Crossing the landscape through rivers and mud, Rain tried to drown them and humidity was crud. But they never gave up, a devoted team, they followed their orders even when times were lean.

PTSD-NO APOLOGIES

Bombs falling and mortars firing, each skirmish was very tiring. But they pushed on and on, And little by little they won.

Great evil was done every day, our soldiers saw it in every way. Some minds were strong and handled it well, others never recovered, their minds and fell.

The war ended and soldiers came home, some whole, some mended, and some never to roam. Now it's called PTSD, and there's no apology, just some broken men with broken homes.

Treatment improves every day, the government has gone out of its way. Great hope for normal life has returned, Life's lesson has hopefully been learned.

So let's cheer our soldiers and the red, white, and blue, raise our flag high and respect it anew. Let optimism be the rule, and our planet Earth be our crowning jewel.

3

EVENTUALLY IT ALL FADES INTO NOTHINGNESS

Gerald "Dino" McGrath

As told to Cindy Smith

In 1963, I was drafted into the Army. In August 1965, I landed in Nha Trang, Vietnam. We were fighting against farmers with rifles.

Then we were taken to the base camp near An Khe, thirty-six miles inland from the coastal city of Qui Nhon. Camp Radcliff.

The 1st Calvary Division unit was called in to relieve 7th Calvary Division who was fighting in the La Drang Valley, called the "Valley of Death". It was the first big battle of the Vietnam War. Those boys had been hit pretty hard. So many soldiers were wounded or dead. North Vietnamese regulars were trained soldiers; they were not the farmers we had been fighting. This was a brand new game for us.

I was shot and wounded in the battle. I

was due to be released in December of 1965, so I was sent home.

When I came back to the States, I just didn't want to be around people. I drove all the way from Chicago to Florida just to be alone, to get away from people. The people protesting the war. And, I guess it worked for a while.

Time heals all wounds, so they say. *Eventually it all fades into nothingness.* But, I know it was all real. It just continues to pop into your head every now and then.

But you can't spend your time thinking about it.

I was diagnosed with PTSD a few years ago. You were seeing things over there you didn't need to see. That's what stresses you out. I still have nightmares to this day. I never know when they will occur. The dreams feature a man who is charging me with a bayonet. I'm in a dark hole, and can't get out. The man stabs me through the neck. There was one night my wife woke me up. My hands were around her neck, I was choking her and she had no idea what I was doing! She didn't appreciate that at all. In fact, I had to spend the rest of the night on the couch.

At first, The VA gave me some pills to help with the PTSD. They were just a fancy name for nothing more than sleeping pills. So, I stopped taking them.

I tried locating and contacting other Army buddies, just to see how they were and how they were doing. You know, for old times' sake. Most do not want to talk to you. They do not want to be bothered, do not want to socialize; mostly they just want to left alone. Maybe they want to forget.

I occasionally drive hundreds of miles to visit an old Army buddy in West Virginia. I enjoy talking with him, and his wife. For me, this is the best medicine, better than any pills the VA could give you.

They made a movie about the battle at La Drang. Mel Gibson was in it. It was called, "We Were Soldiers". Of course, it's the Hollywood version. So, how do I get through each day, you ask? It's a choice. I guess... I just choose to be happy. It's all you can do.

ANDERSONVILLE

Poem by Lynn Hubbard

The Southern Flag Flies
As we lay in the dirt
The walls are 15 feet high
We are dying from thirst.

Brother Verses Brother
Well he ain't no kin to me
This War is a hard one
We just want to be free

The trains roll in like waves
Carrying misery and grief
Enough is enough already
We can' get no relief

Sun beats down day and night
There is no place to sleep
No water from the foul creek
'Cause the mud is thigh deep

No shelter or clothing
Flies buzz in our heads
Sickness runs rampant
The lucky ones are dead

They called it Andersonville
A name no one should forget
It is emblazed on our souls
It took a heavy debt.

RURAL ROUTE

Art by Kerry "Doc" Pardue

6

KEEP YOUR BACK TO THE WALL

Anonymous

Just suppose, you live in your own little corner of hell. Everyday.

It is full of monsters and demons, the kind that would make anything in the movies seem like cheap Halloween tricks. They come mostly at night. Mostly. But you have known them so long that now they don't frighten you anymore. At least not like they used to. They are almost your friends. You sure don't have any others. At least you know where you stand with them. They weave in and out of your sleep. Maybe the worst part is sometimes it's hard to tell if you are asleep or awake. What is real?

The night terrors are still there, but they are easier to cope with. It's not because you know they can't hurt you, but because you just don't care anymore. You don't sleep much until the sun starts coming up. Then you think it may be safer, at least until dusk.

Oh, you want to hear war stories and nightmares? Sorry, they are mine and they are private. Besides, you don't really want to be in my head.

During the day, you still have to be vigilant. If you are out somewhere, you need to sit in a corner, or at least with your back to a wall. You don't want anyone to be able to get behind you. Check-out lines where you are shopping can be bad. If people start getting too close it makes you nervous. You have to avoid confrontations if possible. Not because you are afraid of what someone might do to you, but of what you might do to them.

So you try to stay in your own world and let everyone else stay in theirs. I once heard it said that if you look into the abyss too long, it will start looking back into you. Well, have at it! I have been doing it for almost 50 years and I am still here and I still have my sanity. The rest of the world is crazy. Most of the people I know are pathetic, helpless creatures that couldn't find their own ass with both hands and a flashlight.

The men, just boys really, who were "there" could be counted on. You knew they could take care of themselves and would not hesitate to help you. Most of the people we came back to only use other people. Oh sure, they may do something for you, but only to serve their own ends. If you ask someone you have known for a long time and you thought cared something about you for help that does not cost anything and only would require a few minutes occasionally, chances are they won't take the time to do anything for you unless it is something that they want to do for themselves. Even if it is something they have done many times before. It's like they won't do it just because it would help you and you need it. But when they want you to do something....

And the Drs. wonder why we don't trust anyone. Or maybe that's just the type of people I always ended up associating with.

Once the VA decides to treat you for PTSD, they send you to a Psychiatrist who often times were raised in another country, another culture. They ask about your childhood and other things that they would have no comprehension of. How can they relate to anything in your past? They will load you up with drugs to the point that you can't function. Once, I told my VA Psychiatrist I could not function on my medication.

I could not drive or concentrate. Could not form coherent thoughts. She said we need to increase the dose. So she doubled my medication. You can imagine how that worked out. I have known other veterans with the exact same experience. It's like the Drs. think they can medicate us into oblivion. I don't know if that's the Dr.'s idea or if the VA encourages them to medicate us to the point that all we can do is sit and drool all over ourselves (I know many other vets who have had the same experience with different VA Drs.). I, along with many of the other vets no longer take any anti-depressant or anti-anxiety medications. Some that do take the meds take only half or quarter doses. One of my friends goes to two psychiatrists, one a VA Dr. and the other a private Psychiatrist. He was having a lot of problems with his meds. The private Dr. looked at his medication list and told him he was way over medicated and to just to quit taking what the VA Dr. had prescribed. Get the prescription filled and let them think you take it, but you will be better without it. And it worked. He can now function pretty much on a normal level.

When I came back from Vietnam all I wanted to do was put it behind me. We were looked down on and no one wanted anything to do with us. After all, we were a bunch of "baby killers". That is probably what gave us the "I don't need you" attitude. Then a strange thing happened. I don't really remember the exact time frame, maybe late 70's or early 80's, people started claiming to be Vietnam Vets who had never even been in service. They bought surplus clothing, dressed like vets and told war stories. Maybe it was guilt because they didn't go. They finally realized that they were a bunch of chicken-shit assholes who were too concerned with their own personal safety to serve their country. Not that being in Vietnam was right. With the benefit of hindsight, the United States should not have been involved in a civil war half way around the world. But once we were in it, "Duty Calls" as they say. The soldier only goes where he is told and fights who he is told to fight. Vietnam was just like Iraq, somebody got rich while we were dying. There's a hot corner in hell for those politicians!

Now people say "Thank you for your service". I am glad that today's veterans actually get that. While some people may be sincere with that comment, it usually rings hollow for me. Sometimes even to the point of being a slap in the face. It's more like "Thanks for going so I didn't have to". Or "Thanks for going so my kids didn't have to." A "politically correct" thing to say. Just more bullshit. I read where the salute to the troops that you see at the beginning of NFL football games that is supposed to be so inspiring is really bought and paid for. The Armed Forces (Army, National

Guard, etc.) actually pay the NFL teams to do the little 1-2 minute salute to the troops before the game. If that's true for the NFL, it's probably the same for MLB, NASCAR, and every other entity who takes the time to "salute" the troops. Thanks a fucking lot.

I guess part of the problem is that not everyone who serves their country returns with the same frame of mind. Some do their duty and put it behind them. Good for them. Unfortunately, some embrace the warrior mentality. They had it before they served. They just didn't know what it was. I read once that in ancient China they segregated the warriors from the general population because they were different. The rulers understood that they were necessary, but did not fit in with "polite" society. Highly trained, willing and able to do what lesser men could not. Not understanding the concept of "can't". Under all the bullshit public displays - NO ONE LOVES A SOLDIER TILL THE ENEMY'S AT THE GATE!

If you think I am bitter, you are wrong. I

am just a realist. That's the ways things are. But sleep well America, I and many like me would still pick up a weapon and defend your right to let better men than yourselves protect your way of life.

>One of Many
>USMC Vietnam '66-'67
>SEMPER FI

7

ANDY BERRY, AMERICAN HERO

By Charlie May

Andy Berry was a true American Hero. His story goes something like this.

Andy was in the Army during World War II. He was wounded two times and received the Purple Heart, and Oak Leaf Cluster and a Silver Star for bravery. There was a bond between me and Andy that I couldn't explain, and within a few days of meeting each other, we had become very close.

In Sicily, a man named Leo Delahay was mortally wounded in battle, his insides were splattered about. Andy Berry left no man behind. He went back and carried Leo to safety. Andy had to crawl half a mile before he was able to stand, the enemy was everywhere. He was a protector, a leader. It followed him into civilian life, he protected everyone.

During the invasion of Normandy, there were 265 men in Andy's squad when they reached the beach. Only 65 of them made it across. Andy was one of the lucky few.

In France, he said they had landed on a beach under fire. They were outnumbered and he heard someone say, 'Retreat'! He said he looked behind him and there was the ocean. There was nowhere to go. Andy said, "Where to? The water?" He was a squad leader and machine gunner so he opened fire with the machine gun and took out the whole company of Germans. Andy held his post, stationed with a lone machine gun, as the enemy tried to drive back his company. He held out the unit until they were able to regroup. For this, Andy received the Silver Star.

He was offered the rank of Sargent, but turned down the advancement. He didn't want to give up his machine gun duties. The machine gunner spot was at the front line of defense. Many didn't live long as a machine gunner.

Andy was awarded two Purple Hearts in the service, and received the Texas Distinguished Service Medal.

Months later, after our first meeting on a concert tour through New York and Virginia, I told Larry (Barrett), I couldn't wait to get back home. I was going to Texas to spend more time with Andy Berry.

I stayed with Andy and his wife, Birdie, for

about three weeks, and we became like family. Andy was such a humble man and he reminded me a lot of my granddad. They treated me like I was their son. They lived in a housing project and couldn't afford to have cable TV. That bothered me, he was a war hero! But, Andy's nephew had given him a DVD player. I think Andy and I sat up every night and watched every old black and white John Wayne movie they ever made on that DVD player.

I loved to listen to his stories. He never let things bother him. The past, the war. He focused on his love for his family instead. I guess he thought there was no need to look back on things you cannot change. He'd talk about the destruction of the war, the way a beautiful forest looked like toothpicks after a bomb had hit it. But, other than that, he spoke positive, let his light shine, and never let anything else show through.

After leaving Texas and getting back home, I wrote and recorded a song about Andy, "Tribute to an American Hero", and sent it to him. It was just before Veterans Day, and his wife took the CD to their church and they played it for him. She called me afterwards to tell me that everyone loved it and some of the comments she heard.

She said a young man came up to Andy and said, "Wow! You're a real hero!" Andy said, "No son, we left the hero's laying in the fields." When I heard what he said, it moved me to write another song in honor of our soldier's that were killed in battle. I called it, "Freedom's Light".

Andy was a special man. A true American hero. I'll never forget him.

THE UNKNOWN SOLDIER

<u>Poem by Lynn Hubbard</u>

He sleeps in the earth
A guardian is near
To keep watch at night
Without any fear

Exactly twenty one steps
Rain, sleet, or snow
No comfort for them
Honor is what they know

Died without a name
But Angels guide his soul
He lives forever in our hearts
He has paid our toll

The Unknown Soldier
Has given his all
To make this land safe
He's not a name on a wall

He is not alone
Others are here
Let's show our thanks
To our Soldiers lying there

9

DANNY'S STORY

As recalled by Author Jon Broderick

During their skiing days from 1969 -1991

Post-Traumatic Stress begins with your first day in training as a recruit in the mind killing schools known as Hell on Earth. Danny Carson was still a teen ager when he showed up after his basic training was completed and he qualified for the school in San Diego where he would learn underwater demolition training, special weapons and warfare skills that were to serve him faithfully, and save his life in a faraway place called Viet Nam.

Danny hadn't killed any other humans yet. But that was soon to change. The breakdown of the human mind and the replacement with a warrior's mindset along with a body trained to kill quickly and efficiently soon replaced the innocent boy that grew up surfing in the ocean and skiing at the Greater Miami Water Ski Club behind the Miami International Airport as a youngster.

Danny, born January 9, 1949, was a decorated Navy Seal, who served three tours of duty in Vietnam, receiving, among other decorations, the Bronze Star and Purple Heart. After his military service, he built a successful roofing company, publishing company, and roofing consulting company. At the pleasure of the Governor, he served for many years on the State Construction Licensing Board. Danny was a dedicated coach to Cypress Lake Hornets Pop Warner Football Team for ten years and served as president for five years. He coached football at Bishop Verot High School for the past two years.

January 1968 Cambodian-South Viet Nam Border

Carson was the point man. His 11 man recon team followed, trying and failing miserably to maintain stealth in the steaming, mosquito infested jungle. Suddenly, monkey chatter silenced. Carson signaled his team to take refuge in the thick jungle. Within seconds the sounds of an approaching squad of Viet Cong soldiers could be heard and they were getting closer. They passed without detecting Carson's squad but found a small river around the next bend and decided to set up camp for the evening. Soon the cooking fires were lit and, thinking no enemy was nearby, the forty-eight, black clad, barefooted members of the raiding party took off their straw hats, ate their meager rations and prepared to sleep.

Four perimeter guards were the first to die silently under the sharp blades of the Navy Seal knives. Their comrades heard nothing. It was just before midnight when twenty more sleeping soldiers woke up with their mouth covered and their throats slit sending them back to sleep forever. But, there was noise, and thrashing. Soldiers stirred, reached for their weapons and were struck with bullets fired from the small band of Seal team marksmen. One Viet Cong remained alive for a few seconds and it was enough to change Danny's life forever.

Carson approached a wounded Cong soldier who rolled over on his back displaying a grenade. He was pulling the handle, causing the igniting spark to detonate the explosive content of the canister. Carson turned his head to the side and hollered for his men to duck just as he hurled his own body at the Cong with the grenade.

A Week Later

The four surviving seals managed to kill the remaining few North Vietnamese soldiers and recover the remains of seven Navy Seals who died in the grenade blast. Carson suffered severe wounds to his neck and to both upper legs as the blast decimated the men directly behind Carson. They carried Carson several miles to the joined tributaries of a river where a rescue operation and evacuation was set up. A support military group had a link to a helicopter extraction unit that flew in and landed on the river delta shore barely avoiding overhanging trees. Flying one of the helicopters during that rescue mission was Lonnie Carson, Danny's older brother.

Danny himself described his injuries and how it happened. The Viet Cong used large soup cans containing gunpowder, bits of broken glass, nails and metal fragments that they packed along with human feces with a little gasoline or diesel fuel for an accelerant. The activator for the suicide bomb was a large stick, covered with flint that, when pulled out of the can quickly, set off sparks when it rubbed against the shreds of any metal.

Not only did the Cong blow himself up, the fragments ripped Danny's throat open and shredded his legs. The exploding bomb created a rather ugly tracheotomy in Danny's neck that provided an airway through which he could breathe. The damages were so severe he would have drowned in his own blood otherwise. The shrapnel from the blast killed the Seals who stood directly behind Carson. His surviving seal team members carried Danny out of the jungle to the river where the medevac helicopter carried Danny and his surviving team members to safety. It was during the trip that Lonnie found out that he was rescuing his own brother.

1971 Cape Coral, Florida

The recollections of Danny Carson's story are from the stories he and Lonnie told me during our years together. Unfortunately, Danny died in a single car accident after suffering long and heartbreaking disasters that led to a downward spiral of his very existence due to the effects of post traumatic syndrome disorder. That Lonnie was unable to contribute many details of Danny's ordeal stems from a nearly fatal helicopter crash while serving as Captain and Chief Pilot for the Lee County Sheriff's Department for over 20 years. He suffered from major head injuries and is medically retired and disabled.

After Danny recovered from his injuries, he married his wife, Marie and moved from Miami to Cape Coral, Florida to assume control over Lee County Metal & Roofing Company, a small roofing contractor that he would eventually buy and turn into a very successful business.

I met Danny when he showed up at a water ski school I was running at the time in Cape Coral at the Yacht Club. Our little club was performing water ski shows on weekends and Danny, a former competitive water skier asked to join our group. Though Danny was fit, he had many scars, and an intense desire to ski and get stronger.

During the months and years that followed, I saw the effects that that grenade had on Danny's body. Anything as mundane as a common cold was potentially fatal for Danny. The pollutants imbedded in that bomb left him with a condition known as severe septicemia. His blood was toxic and devoid of antibodies that could fight infection. When airport x-ray machines were introduced at airports, Danny's image would appear with thousands of little white objects on the x-ray screen from the shrapnel he carried in his body from that blast. I saw Danny get chilled after skiing on a cool winter day and progress from a sneeze to 105-degree fever in the space of 10 minutes.

But, he was tough, and competitive. We water skied together and trained together for several years and enjoyed competing in the tournaments in the U.S. Southern Region. Danny's specialty was water ski jumping and I saw him jump almost 140 feet on several occasion back in the late 1970's.

1980's – 2000

As Danny's professional life grew more and more successful, his demons resurfaced. A lot of the details have been lost as his two daughters and son grew up. Danny abused alcohol from time-to-time, but his real nemesis became cocaine. His nightmares were more frequent. His bouts with depression became more intense and his son, now a young man, was soon following a dangerous path toward drug and alcohol abuse.

Danny's business began to falter, and his relationships with relatives also degenerated. His brother, Lonnie was a captain and chief pilot for the Lee County Sheriff Department in Southwest Florida, and Danny's behaviors compromised the relationship with Lonnie, the man who rescued him in Viet Nam.

Danny was driving alone in the area of Bonita Springs on Interstate 75 when the single car accident took place on January 14, 2000. He slammed into a roadside assistance telephone box along the Interstate. He was driving at a high rate of speed and the call box may have possibly been his target. The details of the Sheriff Department investigation have not been made public, and Lonnie isn't talking.

Danny was a strong man, and a good friend. He carried a load of posttraumatic stress from his three tours. When he went back to claim his military possessions after his recovery, he was distressed because he was not allowed to keep his favorite machine gun, nor his dehydrated collection of human ears that were strung on a belt that wrapped around his waist...twice keeping a grisly score of the prior 48 Viet Cong he had killed before the blast at the enemy encampment.

Danny G. Carson-Obituary

Danny G. Carson, 51 years, beloved husband, father and brother, died of injuries sustained in an auto accident on January 14, 2000. He is survived by his wife, Marie; daughters, Danielle and Heather; son, Bo; sisters, Anita Jinkins and Linda Epling of Miami; brother, Lonnie Carson of Fort Myers; and many nieces and nephews.

Danny, born January 9, 1949, was a decorated Navy Seal, who served three tours of duty in Vietnam, receiving, among other decorations, the Bronze Star and Purple Heart. After his military service, he built a successful roofing company, publishing company, and roofing consulting company. At the pleasure of the Governor, he served for many years on the State Construction Licensing Board. Danny was a dedicated coach to Cypress Lake Hornets for ten years and served as president for five years. He coached football at Bishop Verot High School for the past two years.

Funeral service will be conducted Wednesday, January 19, at 1:30 p.m. at Cypress Lake Baptist Church, 8400 Cypress Lake Dr., with Pastor Danny Harvey officiating. The family will receive friends Tuesday evening from 7:00 to 9:00 p.m. at the Harvey-Engelhardt-Metz Funeral Home, 1600 Colonial Blvd, Fort Myers.

'You will be forever in our hearts and forever with us.'

Published in The News-Press on Jan. 17, 2000

10

YOUR LIFE MADE A DIFFERENCE... TO ME

<u>Poem by Kerry "Doc" Pardue</u>

It has been over 40 years since we served together
We were the hope for our generation
Our 19 – 20 year old bodies and minds
Thought we were indestructible

We went when told to go
Did what others did not want to do
Came home wounded, broken, disillusioned, and despised
And now, mostly forgotten

Jim, I remember your strength, your smile, your bravery
You helped us all in the midst of battle
You never complained or questioned
You were the "Soldier's Soldier"
Several years later I found you on the internet

PTSD-NO APOLOGIES

We spoke like we did to each other back then
Happy to know we made it home
Then the topic changed in our conversations

Some of great joy of children births
Others of failed relationships
Three women tried and failed to stay
Couldn't handle the stress and the rage

The overwhelming nightmares and flashbacks
Failure to let anyone get close again
Fear of losing another one again
Pushing those you loved far away

We lose touch from time to time
Blaming it on busy lives
But something would call us back
To speak and hear a voice from the past who understood

The smell of death, the piles of bodies and parts;
The pools of blood and bandages,
Of knowing real fear and facing it together;

PTSD-NO APOLOGIES

Surviving another night and battle.

I email and call but no answer
Knowing full well the time is not good for you
I offer a word of prayer
A return to my own private world alone.

Then the phone call
Telling me of the note and the pull of a trigger
That ended your life, I am saddened as I could have done more
Damn it Jim, you promised that you would not be a number

You have become a sad reminder of what PTSD
Untreated can do
I wonder are you any better now that you are gone
Seems like a waste, a life of regret, gone unfulfilled

Yours is a number that now is more than double
The names that are on the cold black stone

In Washington, DC

You took a permanent solution to a temporary situation

Your life had value
Your life had real meaning
Your life made a difference
To Me...

11

INVISIBLE

Anonymous

As told to Cindy Smith

Operation Desert Storm began on the 17th of January 1991, at 2:10 am, Baghdad time, when Task Force Normandy (eight US Army AH-64 Apache helicopters led by two US Air Force MH-53 Pave Low helicopters) destroyed Iraqi radar sites near the Iraqi-Saudi Arabian border, which could have warned Iraq of an upcoming attack. The mission was to capture Saddam Hussein and bring down the Iraq's Army, the 4th largest army in the world.

I was a Sergeant in the Air Force from 1981 to 1991, a Desert Storm Veteran. I was a Training Manager. I had several different jobs, but during wartime, I acted as Security Police. The first line of defense at Tabuk Air Station, Saudi Arabia.

It was very hot when we deployed to the

desert. We were in jungle bdu's (battle dress uniforms) so we would blend in. The sand storms were terrible. It was impossible to do anything outside during a sand storm, but you were still expected to do your duty, no matter what. When we walked the security rounds in the sand storms, you could not see your hand in front of your face. The temperatures could exceed over one hundred degrees.

The Commander told us that Saddam Hussein has seven different chemical weapons that we knew of, and Biological Weapons. There was a big possibility that you could be dosed with chemicals at any time. When we were deployed, we only had training suits for chemical warfare from WW2. They are not good for anything, especially war fare. We had air raids almost every night, I'd be sleeping and all of a sudden, wake up. You would never know when one would hit us. We were all stressed the entire time just thinking about it.

In Riyadh, Saudi Arabia, I was close to an explosion. A Scud missile was shot down by an MIM-104 Patriot tactical air defense missile outside of Riyadh. The sandbags - our fallout shelter - was knocked right off and on top of all of us huddled behind it. My ears didn't stop ringing the rest of the day. After that - man it got real! Very real. It was a wakeup call.

I got out of the Air Force soon after Desert Storm. It was mainly due to force reduction. I took a civilian job and went to work. I stayed busy, just trying to get my life back together. At home, my wife told me I had changed. I began having violent dreams. We had two teenage (step) sons, and yes, I admit I did have some problems with them. I just blew it off to the fact that they were teenagers. Now, I think the problem was with me, not them. My marriage ended in divorce. I became withdrawn, didn't want to be around people.

When I went in for my Gulf War screening (at the VA), they did not do any testing for PTSD. They said I had the Gulf War illness and I should go file a claim. But, the way the VA is, it has two different sides. The bureaucrats and medical. It's like two complete different organizations. They put up a brick wall between them and you, then you gotta fight for medical compensations. They send you to appointment after appointment. I was so frustrated; I finally dropped the claim and just went back to work. That's what they hope you will do, give up.

I must have gone through fifteen different jobs between 1991 and 2008. I would get mad, couldn't agree with people, and thought, man, these people are idiots! They didn't understand. I realize now the problem was me, it was my fault. I let the day to day stress get to me.

In 2007, I was officially diagnosed with PTSD. I have the normal array of symptoms, hearing voices in the distance, seeing shadows in the room, seeing lights, like flashlights through the windows. I get rashes, headaches, fatigue. I have hallucinations and sickness.

The problem with the VA is that they will tell you have PTSD, and then they ask YOU how you got it. Ha! It's very frustrating. The doctors will listen to you, and their resolution is to give you pills, and more pills. I have twenty-four different prescriptions. All those drugs will make you a zombie.

I didn't even consider it until now, the things I have seen - maybe not stressing me then because it wasn't happening to me. I was just watching a program on combat rescue and a guy was talking about how it has affected him, and others he knows, seeing the carnage. And, you know he is right. I've seen a good bit of it from the ten years I was in. One example being; I had to pick up scattered body parts from a plane crash. It was way before the war, but still it's something that keeps lingering inside your mind. There are so many things that can contribute to PTSD. You just never know what will surface.

My mind isn't on Desert Storm every day. I try not to think about it. Trying to voice my thoughts, that is, what I mean to say, is hard for me. My mind gets scrambled with what I'm thinking. I get zoned out watching TV or a movie. The movie will be over and I realize I didn't watch it, can't remember what it was about. I went off somewhere in my mind. I didn't even know it happened.

I don't want my family to worry about me. Don't want my friends to think I'm totally insane. If you're doing a good job, you can hide it. I deal with my problems within myself. The hardest thing is to be judged by others. It's not something you can see with your eyes. Friends and family want to push you to socialize and be around people, I understand that. But, they don't know how I feel. I enjoy staying home in my own little world. For me, it's isolation. The calmness with being alone. I don't focus on the bad. I don't want to be singled out, stigmatized, and looked down on. It's not an easy thing to talk about and I don't want anyone to judge me. I don't judge anyone. Civilians don't understand. They were not there. So, I just go to that happy place in my mind.

The PTSD thing - to admit you have it makes you feel guilty. That's why most guys won't talk about it or admit they have it. You can see the guys with physical disabilities, no arms, no legs, head injuries ...but with PTSD, if you hid it well, it's invisible. You compare yourselves to them, and what you have is like nothing. If you can't see it, then maybe it's not there, it doesn't exist.

I have a friend with PTSD who drinks to escape his demons. That's the way he handles it. I read about the suicides of all the Vets. The way they are handled by the VA system, it's no wonder they are hanging on the edge. You are diagnosed with PTSD by the doctors, but (if you're like me) you're not getting any compensation. You're living on less than $600.00 a month. It's enough to push you over the edge. I don't believe in suicide. It's not the way out, but I understand. You just can't give up.

By the way, my PTSD claim with the VA, is STILL pending.

FREEDOM'S LIGHT

<u>Song by Charlie May</u>

I hear the sound of angels, flying overhead.
They're coming here from Heaven, to take back our dead.
Now the battlefields are bloody, where our soldiers lie
And the Lord said go get my children, as their spirit start to rise.

Go get my children and bring them back to me,
The war is over and their souls have been set free.
They fought the battle bravely, now the day in done.
Freedom's light will never die because the victory has been won.

No greater love then a man lay down his life for his friends.
This is dedicated to the men and women of The

United States Armed Forces, who fought and died, that others might live free.
The world saw your courage, there at Flanders field, you showed
The meaning of sacrifice and some lie there still.

They hit you hard at Pearl Harbor and thought you'd surely fall
But at Okinawa and Iwo Jima, they found you standing tall.
When Korea, Vietnam, and the Middle East made their plea full cry.
Once again you answered the call with Ole Glory flying high.

You carried out your duty, in the air and land and sea
And because of men and women like you, this country is still standing free.
Go get my children and bring them back to me,
The war is over and their souls have been set free.

They fought the battle bravely now the day in done.

Freedom's light will never die because the victory has been won.

Blessed are the peacemakers, for they shall be called the children of God.

13

I AM NO STRANGER TO PTSD

Ron Asby

I guess you would say I come from a lineage of "patriots". "Patriots", meaning those who love this country and served in the military for our freedom. Grandpa Ben, WWI veteran; Uncle Harry, Uncle Bill, Uncle Billy and my Dad, WWII veterans. All of these men were my idols growing up. The last thing I ever wanted to do was disappoint them.

I am coming clean.....I was a draft dodger. I graduated High School in 1965 and went to college. After three semesters of not studying and having "way too much fun," I lost my coveted draft deferment. After classes one day in January 1967, Mom met me at the front door and said "You have mail on the television." I could sense the melancholy and apprehension in her voice. The letter was staring at me and daring me to open it.

I knew what it was from the return address. I hastily opened it and scanned the text...."you are to report to the induction center on....." The Viet Nam War was raging in some far off place, I was scared and rushed out of the house clutching the letter. I hopped on my motorcycle and "beat feet" to the US Navy recruiting office. I tossed the letter to the recruiter and asked "can you help me?" The rest is history. I spent the next 6 years in the US Navy as an Electronics Technician. A patriotic way to dodge the draft wouldn't you say? My Navy service is one of my proudest accomplishments.

During the 60's and 70's three of my cousins (US Army), my middle brother (US Navy) and a future brother-in-law (US Air Force) all served our country during the Viet Nam War. Years later our son Ben (USMC, Operation Enduring Freedom, Afghanistan), a nephew (US Air Force, Afghanistan and Iraq), a nephew-in-law and his brother (both USMC, Operation Iraqi Freedom) served in the USMC.

I am no stranger to those close to me

suffering with Shell Shock/PTSD. My Uncle Billy was bayoneted and left for dead on Guam in 1943. He was the only survivor of his platoon. Uncle Billy was an alcoholic, wife abuser, and child abuser after the war. I actually hated him for what he did to my aunt and especially my girl cousins. It wasn't until I was in my thirties that I realized his problems were a result of his WWII experiences (Shell Shock as it was called back then). I finally made peace with Uncle Billy when he was in his 70's. He passed away just two week before he and Dad were scheduled to take an Honor Flight to Washington D.C.

Our son Ben suffers from PTSD. It took eight years for him to open up to the family on his actions in Afghanistan. He came home angry, combative and abusing alcohol. He can't sleep due to nightmares. After much urging by his mother and me, he got into the VA system and was diagnosed with PTSD but denied a disability because he could hold down a job.

Thankfully he reapplied and was awarded a

disability for PTSD. He is getting help now from the VA. His therapy is mostly medication and that has its own problems. In 2014 the VA (under a lot of pressure) granted him approval for a service dog program. Ben was accepted into a service dog program and placed on a one year waiting list. He finally attended training and received his service dog in 2015 at a not-for-profit program in Florida. So far the results are promising, especially at night. His dog senses his nightmares and lays on him to comfort him.

Service dogs are a relatively new therapy for PTSD and TBI (Traumatic Brain Injury). The VA is slow to adopt new therapies. The American Legion is taking the forefront in lobbying congress to have the VA reconsider alternative therapies.

North Cobb American Legion Post 304 has made combating PTSD a priority in our outreach to veterans in need. We have partnered with a not-for-profit in Georgia that trains service dogs specifically for veterans with PTSD/TBI. The service dogs are typically rescued dogs. The cost to the veteran is zero but the training is costly. Post 304 raises funds to cover the cost of the training and veterinary fees. It is a win-win, helping veterans and saving dogs from possible euthanasia and a new purpose. We will make a difference.

We owe these veterans every opportunity to combat the demons that haunt them. They have sacrificed for our country, us and our freedom. The least we can do is contact your congressman, and make a donation for the training of service dogs.

Ron Asby, Commander
North Cobb American Legion Post 304
Acworth, Georgia

14

INVISIBLE SCARS

<u>By Lynn Hubbard</u>

Some scars are hidden
Deep inside our hearts
Invisible to others
But they tear us apart

You were not even there
So how can you judge?
That my fears are not real
So onward I trudge

In silence I live
Not saying a word
But the pain inside
Screams to be heard

I am not normal
Everyone has flaws
I can never return
To who I once was

One day at a time
Is all that I ask
Until I can conquer
My haunted past

Life has changed me
I am different these days
But I will survive
In my own way

Scars make us stronger
We have thicker skin
But you are not alone
Let someone in

15

I EXIST TO LIVE

Hugh Lee Young

As told to Cindy Smith

I was born in Roopville, Georgia in 1923. At 91 years old, I believe I am the only living WWII POW in Carroll County, Georgia.

I flew in the Army Air Corps with the 376th Heavy Bombardment Squadron. I went overseas at twenty-one years old. I flew in twenty-seven combat missions and it was on the twenty-seventh mission that I was shot down.

My B-24 plane was shot down over Northern Italy on December 28, 1943. The B-24 Heavy Bomber, nicknamed the "Flying Boxcar", was built around a central bomb bay that could accommodate around eight thousand pounds of artillery in each of its forward and aft compartments. I was ball turret gunner. The ball turret was a bubble on the bottom of the plane, being the first line of protection for the plane while flying on missions. I was curled up in a small confined space for the duration of the flight. I couldn't wear a parachute in there, it was the coldest (often times below freezing) and the most dangerous position in the plane.

The day we were shot down, the plane caught fire and it burned my face. We were soon captured on the ground. They weren't too nice towards me 'cause I got a German name. They wanted information, I didn't know anything. I was captured and sent to Frankfort, Germany and they put me in confinement. Then they transferred me to a POW Camp near Clems, Austria, forty miles north of the Danube River. Stalag 17-B, a German prisoner of war camp.

When I went in, I weighted over 160 pounds. When I left, I was just about 115 pounds. There were over 3200 prisoners in that camp. Just looking at the countryside, you would think it was such a beautiful place. But, it was definitely not like that on the inside. We slept on straw, bug infested make-shift mattresses, three men high. There were guards with machine guns all around us, night and day. If any one of us went outside of our barracks after dark - they were shot no matter what. I remember one man lost his head one night, ran outside in the dark. He was shot and killed and left there hanging on the barb-wire fence until morning, for a warning to all of us.

There wasn't enough food to feed all of us, we mostly ate a thin soupy broth that you weren't even sure what it was. It was better not to think about what was in it. Once we caught a duck, and roasted him for dinner. It smelled so good that the guard caught a whiff of it and wanted a piece. I told him he could have a piece if he gave me a slice of bread. He went and came back with a slice of bread. That was amazing to me that I could bluff a guard into doing something like that.

The Russian prisoners were next to us, just over a barbed wire fence. If we thought we were treated badly, the Russians had it worse! One day, there was a Russian hanging out near the fence. I thought I'd do something nice, and threw a bar of soap over the fence to him. Of course, they hadn't had a bath since they'd been in there, and I felt really bad for them. The soap bars were really small and came in a Red Cross package. The prisoner caught it, but never seeing anything looking like that before, he thought it was food. He brought it up to his mouth and tried to eat it! Then, he shook his fist at me, and in Russian words I couldn't understand, started yelling and (I presume) cussing at me! That's still funny when I think about it.

You see that picture on the wall? That's my POW picture they took the day I got there. I was in the office one day and accidentally found the cabinet where they filed them. So, I "borrowed" mine and a couple of other fellows I knew. If I would have been caught, they would have shot me. I saw some people shot for less than that.

There were some people who tried to escape. The most creative attempt was some fellows using a tape measure and a notebook. I guess they were gonna measure their way right out of camp.

It was April 8th, 1945, the day the gates swung open and we were liberated and were able to walk out. Three days after the war ended. When we walked by the gas chambers and looked in the windows, where the Nazis' slaughtered all those Jews, I couldn't begin to tell you what that smelled like. It was unbelievable.

When it was all over, we came back to the United States on a boat. When we saw the Statue of Liberty, all the men saluted at the site of it. I traveled back to Georgia by train. When they asked me if I wanted to sign up again, I said, "Are you kidding?" I was a POW for two years, eleven months and seventeen days.

For my service, I received the Purple Heart, the POW medal, the Distinguished Service Medal and 18 other medals. There was one act that I didn't receive a medal for, but it was the only thing I would say that I deserved a medal for. Everyone on the plane had a job to do. I was the ball turret gunner. It was tight quarters, not much room in there to move around with the machine guns. But, on one mission, I just happened to notice the bomb propellers were hooked up to go the wrong way. The bombs had arming wires with propeller driven fuses. *(The propellers armed the bomb to detonate after a certain number of revolutions. The propellers started turning after the bomb was dropped from the aircraft.)* We were twenty-thousand feet in the air. I walked out on the catwalk, it was cold, narrow and not enough room to wear a parachute. It was a jumble of wires, cables, and hydraulic lines. This would normally be done using a five minute oxygen mask. But, I didn't have one. I just went out there and stopped the propeller with my hands, no gloves. I switched the wires to make them go the right way. One wrong move would have been the end to it. I was out there long enough to die from the lack of oxygen. Then, someone came out there and gave me an oxygen mask to put on. The bombs were eventually dropped where they were supposed to, but that could have ended badly for all of us on that plane.

You know that TV show, Hogan's Heroes? Well, they changed it to say Stalag 13 instead of 17. The Commandant was "Kuhn". On the show it was "Colonel Klink". I remember we had one guard there like Sergeant Shultz on the show. He would actually say, "I know nothing, I know nothing!" I guess if you were to ask which character I was like on the show, it would be Sergeant Carter (Larry Hovis). He was the southern one with the dog. That was a good show. But, of course, it was nothing like what really happened.

When I came home, yea, it was a little hard to adjust. I had married my sweetheart, Mertha, while I was on leave. We had two children. We were married almost seventy years before I lost her. I had the nightmares. I still do - every once in a while. I once kicked my wife out of bed while having a nightmare. That was something you don't do twice!

I didn't used to talk about the war or camp. All those years, I just never talked. You didn't hear about PTSD back then. That kind of stuff wasn't talked about.

The turning point for me was back a few years ago. I was in Roopville attending the funeral of a man that was also a POW. His sons came up to me after the funeral and said their daddy never talked about the war. They didn't know anything, and asked if there was anything I could tell them. For some reason, I don't know why it happened then, but I told them I would tell them everything they wanted to know.

I told them stories, and then they asked me to come to their school and talk. I did, and now I've been going to the schools here twice a year and speaking to the graduating classes. Then, speaking with their parents at the High School about a career in the Army. I guess the talking about it helps. It does for me.

Before then, I didn't live, I existed. Now I exist to live.

And, I'll be talking until I can't talk no more.

Hugh Lee Young-Now, and the photo that was taken during his POW captivity.

16

NO MORE

Art by Bartholomew Gray

17

DON'T LET IT GET THE BETTER OF YOU

David Silfer

As told to Cindy Smith

Note: I interviewed David Silfer by phone from his hospital bed in early May, 2015. He was limited to speaking only a few minutes at a time. He was on oxygen, coughing, weakened by his illness, but nonetheless, wanted to share his story. David had Stage 4 inoperative cancer in his arm, lungs, spline and liver. I am honored to have had the chance to talk with David. I wish I could have met him and his wife, Ginny. David passed away May 16, 2015 at 6:32 PM surrounded by friends and family. Thank you to his friend, PGR member, Roman Bulkiewicz USMC, for helping to insure his story was told.

I was born in Charleston, Illinois and

graduated from high school in 1969. I started college soon afterwards, took a few odd and end jobs, but could not make ends meet. Times were hard. In January of 1970, I enlisted in the Navy. I took a little flak from family members, they wanted me to join the Air Force instead. I didn't tell them I was thinking about the Navy. I'm a Vietnam era Vet, but I did not go to Vietnam.

I stayed in for four years. Got out in January 1974, almost to the day of enlistment.

I had the nightmares and such, I wasn't immune to the bad dreams. I had issues after I got out, the late night stuff, you know.

Other than picking on a bunch of people, what I do best, (laughing), I think you just got to deal with it, be part of it. Keep your noise above the water. Don't let it get the better of you and pull you down. Because it can - it will take you down in a heartbeat.

I married Virginia (Ginny), my wife, on January 23, 1983. We have one son, Devon Charles, born April 9th, 1993. He's a miracle baby. Ginny and I had been trying a long time to have a baby. Then he arrived.

I was out setting flags for a flag line with the PGR (Patriot Guard Riders) on a mission a few months ago. I felt some pain in my shoulder and walked back and sat in the car. On the 27th of February, 2015, I saw my doctor about the shoulder pain.

I thought I had a pulled muscle, or stress of a pinched nerve, or something like that. However, the tests showed a mass in my lung. The doctor said it was too large to operate. After more testing, they discovered it had already spread to my bones, my arm, my lungs, my liver and my spline. The doctors do not know how long it had been there, or how long I have left. I have Stage 4 inoperative cancer.

At this time, David rested, while Ginny continued the interview.

I come from a large military family and I noticed in civilian life, David was the protector. He was always keeping a watchful eye out everywhere. As a husband, he did everything. The driving, paying the bills, everything. But, he let me be who I was. I worked as a waitress at a truck stop. He taught our son to use gun safety, which is important in the military life style.

He had the nightmares. He would be thrashing around in bed. I would lightly stroke his arm. I couldn't understand what he would be mumbling. For a long time, he didn't talk about this time in his life. He told me, when he came home, he didn't want anything to do with other Vets. I don't know if that's part of PTSD or not.

I pushed him to do the volunteer work. David joined the Patriot Guard Riders and became a ride captain and was a member of the Black Tiger Honor Guard. He joined the American Legion where he served as Past Senior Vice Commander and Past Junior Vice Commander of the American Legion Post 88.

Veterans need to know that we, as Americans, appreciate their sacrifice. David may shake their hands or tell them we appreciate their service, but sometimes I do not know what to say to them. It's hard to find the right words.

That PTSD that they're suffering with, they did this for me. For all of us.

On May 21, 2015, five days after the passing of David Silfer, Roman Bulkiewicz USMC, sent me this Facebook post from Ginny.

My nightly posts these past four months have served as a purge for me – a release of thought and emotion which allowed me to clear my mine and to sleep. Some were written in minutes while others took hours it seemed. I realized tonight that I had one last post to make. It continues from May 16, 2015, 3:39 p.m.

"Death comes in its own time, in its own way and is as unique as the individual who is experiencing it. Please pray for peace for my husband and keep our family in your prayers"... and so it was, his journey ended. After a long visit with his sisters, they left for supper and I noticed that Dave appeared calmer with his breathing so slow & relaxed. He knew his older sister, Pam Kearns, had come to take care of him and I think this was such a reassurance for him, maybe even his unfinished business. Just hours later, at 18:36, he very gently took his last breaths and his physical body was empty. Hospice was called and as we waited for his nurse to arrive, we had well over an hour to cry, come to peace, pray and just be with David before they took him away. As we waited, my sister's minister from the Nazarene church and a dear friend arrived not realizing that Dave had passed and was still in the house. We were gathered around his bedside and said prayers as we cried some more.

This journey began on Feb. 18th because Dave's arm and shoulder hurt while posting flags with some PGR brothers at Danville National Cemetery. X-rays in February showed the lung mass. In March he was hospitalized, had the PET scan and cancer diagnosis. Radiation and chemo treatment in April and finally his death just days ago in May. This has been the most incredibly difficult, heart wrenching, heart breaking experience of my entire life. I'm grateful God gave us these extra days together. Just four short months. For those who may not know, Dave and I met and married within 4 months; and that (at the time) seemed incredibly long!

Please know, I could not have made this journey, with any semblance of sanity, without my faith in our Lord above and all of you. I am beyond blessed to have had the support of such great and wonderful friends from the 32 years of our marriage and the friends and family that drove hundreds of miles to be with me. From the moment I exited the vehicle at Schilling, I and the family who drove me there, were met and escorted to the front doors by a PGR brother.

The dignity, honor and respect displayed during David's visitation at Schillings by the Patriot Guard Riders, The Black Tiger Honor Guard, and the VFW Honor Guard was so very moving. These are the moments that live in your heart forever as it will mine. – I thank God for you all and I may not say it often enough, please know, you each have my love and gratitude. I have asked photos taken during this evening be posted in the album I created on FB – I'll look at these someday when I feel stronger and I will remember. Higher than the mountains that I face ... Stronger than the power of the grave... Constant through the trial and the change... It overwhelms and satisfies my soul...And I never, ever, have to be afraid... One thing remains... Your love never fails, never gives up, never runs out on me...

THE DREAM

Poem by Paden Smith

As I was walking down a dark alley one black summer night,
A stranger came out of nowhere and asked me,
Why I had lost my sight.
I said, 'Old fool! I am not blind.
Stay away from me and I'll allow you to live on another day!'

As he stepped out of the shadows, I saw what he was;
An old soldier who had seen his share of blood.
He wondered why I did not join the cause.
I replied, 'They fight for freedom, but die for nothing.'

I began to walk away.
I felt my muscles grow tight.
In front of me was a battlefield, a dying soldier

lay at my feet.

He asked me if he would make it.

I said, 'Probably not.'

He put a letter in my hand, and told me to give it to his wife.

Then I woke up in my dream.

I went to the mirror. The old soldier was in it.

He pointed to my hand.

In it was the unaddressed letter I was holding.

He told me to open it.

The letter said, "Dear Mrs. Smith, I regret to inform you..."

Paden Smith-Coming Home

19

IN AN INSTANT

John Fredericks

<u>The Catalyst</u>

It was Saturday, November 20, 2010. It was a decent day, all in all. I was to start vacation the next day. I was going to go hunting, real hunting, for the first time. I was hoping to get out of work on time, which would be a rarity in my slice of Milwaukee on any Saturday, even in November. When I got to work, I was nearly over-joyed that I would be working with Tim Toth. Tim's a great guy, love him to death, but we were pretty different cops. Tim likes to take his hitches and get home on time. I hated taking hitches, I went out looking to see what I could find on my own, and going home on time just meant less money on paychecks. Personality-wise, politically, in a lot of ways that make the night fly by, we're pretty similar. So I had it made at the start of the shift.

At this point, I had been with the Milwaukee Police Department for eight years. I had spent a few years on an anti-gang squad, been on a couple specialized investigation squads, and had rotated back into "regular" patrol, and became a field training officer. I was experienced. And I was desensitized more than I knew.

Tim and I had just finished a traffic stop but hadn't cleared with dispatch because Tim wanted to make a quick stop at Walgreens. While I waited in the squad, another sector squad got sent to an address not too far from where we were. Dispatch advised that the caller was being chased by a man with a knife who had already been cutting himself. The squad that was sent, Andy Holzem and Freedom Mustafa, had a combined five years on the street, if that. For whatever reason, I had a bad feeling about that call, and wasn't going to let the new guys fend for themselves.

After what seemed like an eternity, Tim

came back to the squad and I let dispatch know we were going. As we screamed up Capitol Drive, Bradley Tremblay, working the district traffic car by himself, fell in behind us, and we leap frogged our squads through red lights, protecting each other from cross traffic.

As we came to a stop we raced each other to the door of the apartment building. I won and found the front door locked. I could hear Andy yelling commands to an unseen person, "Drop the knife! Drop the knife!"

I pulled out my expandable baton and pounded on a window, to no effect. Seconds later, a kid about 12, dressed in pajamas, let me in and ran out of the building.

I walked into the building's hallway and saw Officer Willie Swims there, pointing a taser at the subject I could now see. The suspect was standing about 18 - 20 feet away, holding a knife. Andy continued to give commands for him to drop the knife, the suspect only responded, "Fuckin' shoot me!" I told Willie to taze the guy already, he told me, "I am man, he's walking through it!" Sure enough, the taser's leads (the wires connecting the taser to the darts that make contact with the bad guy) were attached to the suspect's shirt. Willie pulled the taser's trigger again, and sure enough, nothing, though I could hear the taser's tell-tale clicking that it was doing its job. It had zero effect.

I walked up behind Andy, who was pointing his pistol at the suspect, yelling the same commands and getting the same response. The suspect was taking baby steps forward, towards us. Andy was standing behind a wall where the hallway the suspect was in opens up into the foyer of the building. I took up position on the other side of the foyer opening, pointing my pistol at the suspect. I chose this position because the hallway had jags behind the suspect, and we had no idea what was behind him. This was as good of a position as we could get. We didn't know where the caller was, or what condition she was in. Retreating was not an option, nor was letting the suspect disappear. To do so would leave him the options of hurting or killing the caller or taking her hostage, let alone whoever was in whatever apartments or in the building. Whatever was going to happen was in his hand; we just had control over where it was going to happen.

As I took position, the suspect focused on me with eyes that were somehow simultaneously vacant and determined. I yelled the same commands Andy had been yelling, and gotten the same response. I don't know if it was just my perception, but he seemed more agitated with me. Perhaps it was my imagination, perhaps he was frustrated with my lack of originality. I don't know. I never will.

He kept advancing with his baby steps. He was fixated on me, never taking those eyes I couldn't read off of me. We continued to yell the repetitious dialogue at each other. He kept coming.

We are trained in the Tueller Drill. This is the 21-foot guideline. It states that 21 feet is the distance a normal person can easily cover before an officer can draw his holstered pistol. Any person with a club or edged weapon is in the fatal zone. It's a guideline, not a rule. Our suspect was much closer.

My finger moved to the trigger. Repeating orders back and forth. I remember thinking, "OK, he's about to make up our..." The rest of that thought would have been "minds." But I didn't get to finish the thought. As I thought those words, he took a normal sized step towards us, and was now close enough to jump on us. With no conscious command to my hand, I fired three rounds.

I watched the first round take a leisurely stroll through the air and connect with the left side of his chest. He bent slightly forward and to his left. The second round was much faster but I "saw" it fly into the center of his chest. His knees buckled. I did not see where the third round went, but he fell straight back. I was completely unaware that Andy had also fired a round.

Behind the subject, a woman emerged from a doorway and screamed. I brought my pistol up on the new "target," and ordered her back into the apartment. I've thanked God more than once that I didn't mistakenly perceive her as a threat.

The suspect was lying on his back, his feet towards us. His right arm was propped up by the wall, and its hand still clutched the knife. I felt a hand on my shoulder, and was only then aware that Willie, Tim, and Brad, whose hand was on my shoulder, bringing me back into reality from my moment of... I don't know, reevaluation?

I started moving towards the laid out suspect. I knew he was hit, but didn't know how bad. I had seen two rounds hit "center mass," but also watched him be unphased by the taser. Andy walked behind me, covering downrange, as we're trained, both of us surrendering to training. As I came upon him, I realized there was no way to get that knife out of his hand safely; if he was playing possum, I was open to knife attack. Deciding to risk my leg over my arm (strangely, unconsciously I was really risking my crotch) I kicked the knife out of his hand. Then I looked at his face, which was partially destroyed in the lower right jaw area, and then watched a huge halo of blood around his head expanding.

Though utterly unqualified to *officially* make the decision I officially made, I knew there was no point in performing any rescue techniques, he was dead. I walked to the front door to let the fire department in, as much as to get away from the corpse I just created. Thankfully the other cops, every one of them with less experience, remembered that the job wasn't done, and that we are required to try to help the suspect. They knew what I knew, but had better presence of mind to perform their duties.

The suspect never went to the hospital. He was dead.

In the next hour, I was passed to two sergeants before finally being handed off to Detective Jeremiah Jacks, who was tasked to interview me. I suppose I was technically in custody, and had the right to remain silent, but no one could shut me up as I recounted the events at lightning speed. Jeremiah was kind enough to let me rattle, most likely incoherently, get it out of my system, before getting down to business and getting the investigation going.

At some point, I was able to call my parents and my wife.

The next few hours were a lot of questioning and procedures. I eventually got home. I was terrified to go home. How was she going to see me now? Though I didn't feel any different, I knew I was, that I would never be the same, though I had no idea how that would really be.

When I got home, it was weird, I guess she didn't know what to expect any more than I did. I went over the whole call with my wife and eventually fell asleep as soon as my head hit the pillow.

The Immediate After

Standard deal, three days administrative leave. My phone rang non-stop from the Blue Family. It was great but I had no answer to the question, "How you doing?" I didn't know yet. I was still in the zone, I was still in the mindset of giving my report. I knew, absolutely and unequivocally, that I had done the right thing. If I hadn't shot there was no question in my mind the suspect, whose name I learned at some point, would have been on me or Andy with that knife, no question.

The first day after, I spent the morning pouring through the internet looking for exceptions to the Fifth Commandment, "thou shalt not kill." Though I knew they existed, when your soul is on the line, it helps to get the facts. (It's covered in Catholic Catechism 2265.) We went to one of my brothers' house that day, the whole family had planned to be there for the Packer's game. I retold the tale to all the adults, then again for my dad, a retired Milwaukee Lieutenant of Detectives, and my brothers, two cops and a corrections officer. It was just like the previous night, another investigation, but I didn't mind.

The next day is when I realized I was different when I went to the store because I needed to do something besides sit around the house. People were staring at me. They knew. I had the Mark of Cain upon me. I couldn't get out of the store fast enough, I don't think I bought anything.

On the way back I perceived a car tailgating me on the street. I flipped out. I wasn't right and I couldn't explain it. I just knew that I was wound way too tightly and needed to be away from people.

I was pissed. It made no sense. I did what I had to do, no questions, any way you did the math, I had no choice, and he did! Why did it bother me at all? If I didn't I would be dead.

I went in to work on Monday, not for a shift, but just to see everyone and thank them for the calls and emails and Facebook messages.

Andy and I spent the next couple months working inside while the District Attorney did his investigation and cleared us to go back out on the streets. We got to be friends. We hadn't really talked before, now we were bonded in this experience and forced to be together in the office. We even got a band together.

I used the down time to learn everything I could about the guy I killed, Paul. I learned his criminal history, his prison movements, his driver's license status, and his arrest records. It had been four years since Paul had been released from prison for a string of robberies. He had been taken for mental health evaluation by the Milwaukee Police Department 34 times in that period. Who knows about the suburbs or how many times he went on his own, if he went on his own.

I got copies of the reports. Being homicide reports, I wasn't supposed to have any access to them per policy, but I had friends who just needed to be asked. I studied them, trying to learn about him. I learned why he was at that apartment building: trying to get his landlord, the caller, to get him into a new place. I learned that those who were there that night that knew him described him as a violent man when drinking, which he had been that night. And he hated cops.

I learned from talking to cops who had dealt with him in the past. The previous month he had been taken out to mental health after trying to get a buddy of mine to shoot him, holding his hand behind his back as if he had a weapon.

I got a copy of Brad's squad recording. Brad had his shoulder mic running through the incident. It was 52 seconds between my entering the building to the shots being fired.

I started to feel normal. I hated being inside, I wanted to get back on the proverbial horse, pronto. Andy and I talked about anything and everything but what happened on November 20th.

In late December, my wife and I were a month away from the birth of our second child. Though I was fine, I wanted to get ahead of anything and got the name of a therapist who works exclusively with cops. Wasn't hard to get, we're all crazy. Jay Schrinsky got me in right away. I saw him once and we talked for the hour. He told me about some things people experience; I either didn't have a problem with them or wasn't going through them, so I thanked him and told him I would be in touch if I needed any help.

A few days after Andy and I were cleared by the DA, I was on leave when my son Jack was born. Life was good.

The Next Part

When I got back to work, things went downhill rapidly. I went back to being tightly wound. I fluctuated between what doctor's call "hypervigilance," but is more accurately described as "holy-frickin'-shit-the-war's-about-to-start-vigilance" to periods of what I refer to as "waking blackouts." I don't know what the docs call it. An example: one day I was driving west on W Locust Street, passing N 7th Street. The next conscious thought I had, I was at 31st Street. I have no idea what happened between those points. It happened often. I could not understand it.

My temper was instant. I was getting into it routinely with my supervisors, some of whom enjoyed poking the bear. It was time to get back in touch with Jay.

I got put on a few medications. They kept changing as required, trying to find a good mix.

Problems started developing at home. Not nearly as problematic, I had a temper at home as well. Never got physical, but arguments got more frequent and more heated.

I was having trouble falling asleep. Suddenly I was haunted. In my eight years, I'd been to more homicides than I can recall, add to that fatal accidents. With very few exceptions, I never cared about them any more than was required to do the job. Never lost my appetite, never gave them a second thought. Couldn't. There was just too many.

Suddenly, I was haunted by their faces. Then it got worse. Though I had only witnessed a couple of those homicides as they occurred, I imagined them all happening in ultra-slow motion. There was one that stuck out, probably because it was one of the last homicides I was at, and one that I did not witness.

The story was a woman was dealing marijuana out of her upstairs window. The buyer would pay someone on the street, she would toss the baggies down. One night she offended someone somehow who fired a shot at her, striking her in the cheek, killing her instantly.

In my mind, I was able to see that round first penetrate her skin, then the muscle, then the bone, through the upper palate, through the brain, through the skull, through the scalp. I would see every homicide victim's death in this fashion. Every night.

And when I did fall asleep, I had the same dreams just about everyone reports: replaying that situation or other situations which almost but didn't require the employment of deadly force, only there would be a gun malfunction, bullets just falling out of the pistol to the floor, or some other problem where deadly force was just impossible regardless of the threat.

I see flashes of movement out of the corner of my eye. Hear gunshots only audible to me. Did you know that a gunshot wound to the head has a very distinct smell? I get hit with that smell sometimes.

Why?

I was diagnosed with PTSD, which I thought was bullshit. That's something happens to soldiers in war. I killed one guy who was literally asking for it.

Didn't take long of living that way to realize that the doc, Jim Winston, had to be right. He also gave me a diagnosis of major depression. I didn't have trouble accepting that one.

I think the aspect of this shooting that got to me is that it was a suicide. The term is suicide-by-cop, wherein a person who is unwilling, for any of a wide range of reasons, to pull the trigger himself, provokes an Officer to do the killing for him. The problem for the Officer is that, afterwards, you never know if he was going to follow through with his threat, or if it was an empty threat. It's all hindsight bullshit, but the question of "what if?" has never stopped. If I hadn't shot, would he have dropped the knife and surrendered? It means next to nothing to my brain that, in the moment, in real time, what happened was correct. And I know that given those circumstances 100 times, the result would be the same 100 times.

It does not matter. It wasn't a kidnapper shooting it out with the police, he wasn't a bank robber trying to get away. He had psychological and emotional issues. His true intent can never be known. He left no note. Yes, he carved his arms up before we got there, but, they weren't very deep cuts. I'll never know, and that literally keeps me up at nights to this day.

Unfortunately, things didn't change with the diagnoses. People started getting hurt more frequently and got hit harder than was necessary. I took myself off the street and demanded a transfer after nearly getting into a fist fight with my sergeant. Staying the course was not a safe option for anyone.

Next

I wound up working in an office for a year. Jay Schrinsky told me that I should consider applying for a duty disability retirement. I couldn't even think about it. DDR is for cops who get shot, get into horrible accidents, not for guys who had a bad day.

Word came down that, with everything that had happened, I was never going to be allowed on the streets again. That word came from a member of the command staff who was friendly towards me, and definitely on my side. And I had seen it happen to other cops, I knew that they could do that, and that there was no recourse.

After several months of sitting in a small, glass office, with a busy work job and nothing but time on my hands to think, my night symptoms came into work with me. I applied for the DDR and eventually got it. To my eternal shame.

Life After

My major depression went to suicidal depression.

I found out about a new drug. I had quit

drinking years before, and going back to that wasn't an option. This new drug, named K2 or Spice, was a synthetic marijuana, and it was (at that time) legal. And, like most drugs, the "honeymoon" period was awesome, it really helped the PTSD symptoms and even the depression, though I hated myself for using a non-prescribed drug again. Then it came to a crash, it made the PTSD worse, made the depression worse. I hated myself for "giving up." Hated myself for being unable to do anything about it. I absolutely loathed myself for being a junkie. Then the wife busted me. That sure didn't help anything.

I dug deeper into Paul. More accurately, I kept looking until I tracked down his gravesite. From what I can tell, I'm the only one who visits, though I know both of his parents were still alive as of early 2011.

I don't know that I'm any measure of a success story. I'm still struggling with it. Still symptomatic. Every day is its own struggle. I try to be a good dad. Still suck as a husband. I'm in two bands now, but that isn't as busy as it might sound. I've been chasing God, trying to understand Him as best I can. Trying to do some volunteer work for cops, sponsoring a fellow copper in AA. Keeping up with my meds is key.

If I had advice, it would be to take control of the situation immediately. Don't tough it out. Follow the doc's advice. Take the meds. Don't self-medicate. Stay busy. Above all, I'd tell someone that his/her family needs them, the partners/battle buddies need them to be well. Get a hobby, do something to avoid ruminating on this crap. Be there for people following you down the path. It's not easy, but being in this position is pretty good proof you're not the type to quit anyways. Travel, seek your truth, go fishing, anything is better than letting yourself slip away.

20

LIVING WITH A STRANGER

Rebecca Fredricks

Four years today...four years! Enough to get a Bachelor Degree, or finish high school, to raise a kid to school age. Four years flies by, and drags on interminably, sometimes both at the same time.

Four years ago, I sent my husband to work whole. I went to dinner with my baby girl, my pregnant belly, and my sister, her baby, and her pregnant belly. I missed the first call while I was loading up at the Ruby Tuesday salad bar. My sister didn't miss her call from her own husband, and her face when I walked back told me something was very much up.

Four years ago, he told me was ok when he called again. I believed him. I reassured him, told him I was proud of him, and everything would be ok. He believed me.

Four years ago, he came home after 10 long, silent hours. He smelled of the stress of what he'd been through. He was disheveled and exhausted, his uniform in disarray and his holster empty. Such an obvious missing piece of his uniform, it was as if he were missing a limb. His boots were covered in the dried blood of another man. A dead man, made that way by the conspicuously missing gun. That dead man came home with my husband in every imaginable way: on his boots, in his head, and heavy on his heart.

The man my husband shot was named Paul. I've never met him, never will, but he lives in my house. He lives in my marriage even though he's been dead for four years.

My broken spouse still carries Paul around. He tends to his grave, no one else does. He leaves money on that grave, thinking he will see if someone has been there if the next time he comes, the money is gone. It's still there. I think he hopes (prays?) that someone comes. "Beloved son", the stone says. A beloved son with a rap sheet longer than my arm, extending back to a misguided youth. His parents weren't surprised by how he died, we heard. I'm sure they were broken, too. I'm sure that son was beloved, no matter what. My mother heart cries out for theirs in their loss and devastation.

Four years ago I lost my husband. Paul

took my husband's bullet, and took my marriage, and took the man I expected to raise kids with. He demanded the police "just fucking shoot", and eventually they did. He chose to die at the hand of another. A selfish choice that forces another human to carry the burden Paul could not.

He was fine when he left. I went to Ruby Tuesdays for all-you-can-eat salad, which is a total oxymoron, I say. I had a good life, and a young marriage and growing family. I took it for granted. I never kissed or held the same man again, after he left four years ago. Obviously, my losses are not the same as if he hadn't come home. But, I desperately wish I could have gotten the same man back.

Four years ago, I lost my husband.

I don't think I kissed him goodbye.

21

VIEW OF AN ARMY TRUCK DRIVER

James (Jim) Filhart, United States Army; E5
As told to: Cindy Smith

I served in the United States Army from December 1961 to November 1964. I was stationed for two years in Korea, in peace time, and earned two stripes over there. That wasn't bad. Unfortunately, I was released just six months before the conflicts in Vietnam began.

I saw a lot of stuff over there that still haunts me to this day. There were poor people in Korea, always looking through the trash cans for anything to eat. When I think about it today, especially around Christmas time, it really depresses me. I see how loaded down we are *(here in the United States)* with presents and food, and I remember how they had nothing over there. Of course, that was fifty years ago, and things might have changed, but that's how it was back then.

I drove a semi-truck for the Army. You would see so many people sleeping with their heads on the edge of the blacktop road, trying to stay warmer. It's a wonder I never hit any of them, although I always worried I would. We taught the Korean men to drive the trucks. They couldn't handle the trucks as well as we could from the U.S. At least once a month, one of those guys would hit and run over a child in the road.

The MP's would go and take graphic pictures of the dead child, I mean really explicit, they hid nothing. They would display these photographs at the entrance of the chow line. You would not be allowed to go in and eat without stopping by and looking at the pictures. This was their way of thinking it would make us all better drivers. After a while, it kind of desensitized you. No one ever needed to see anything like that.

In my third year in the Army, when we came back to the U.S., I was hauling a big bulldozer around on a trailer. I saw an elderly couple trying to take an old garage building down all by themselves. It was right across from where we were working. I asked my Platoon Sargent if we could help them, that bulldozer would have finished the job in just a couple minutes. He told me no, we could not help them. If we were anywhere else, outside the U.S.A., overseas, we could. But, it was against policy to help our own people *(civilians)* right here. We had left thousands of dollars' worth of equipment in Korea, and we *(the United States)* spent all kinds of money to help them out, but we can't help out the citizens here when they need it.

I try and stay busy. I'm a member of the Patriot Guard Riders. I do a lot of other volunteer things, including being a DAV *(Disabled American Veterans)* van driver for ten years.

Sometimes this stuff that happened will go through my mind mid-day, other times, at night in my sleep. I have a hard time focusing. My mind wonders off. I do not like going to the VA. I think the VA is passing the buck. I think there is a lot of discrimination going on, about what and who, I won't say. But life goes on, and we have to make the best of it.

THE THINGS THEY CARRY

Art by Chris deRoux

23
THIS STUFF ONLY HAPPENS TO THE LIVING

Ron Papaleoni, USN CPO Retired

Having grown up in an era where the term Post Traumatic Stress Disorder (PTSD) never existed and those suffering with that yet to be named disorder were commonly referred to as having "shell shock" or "soldier's heart". Most folks (mostly military) were labeled as malingerers or cowards. Civilians having the same symptoms were "having an episode" or "nervous breakdown" or just plain crazy. It wasn't until I retired from the military (1981), that the term PTSD became a part of our common language.

My early childhood was filled with getting beaten up at elementary school because I was fat and a "goody-two-shoes". This is what led me to become the class clown. I didn't get beaten as often and actually made some friends. The beatings weren't exclusive to school. My dad was an alcoholic and sometimes would beat me with his belt due to, what he called a "smart ass remark". He was a binge drinker and as such, these incidents were infrequent but memorable not the less. But it was enough for me to move out of the house at 16 and join the Navy at 17.

As we have learned, this documented disorder has been around going back to Egyptian times and mostly involves the military and war. However, as in my case, it is very likely to occur following ANY type of serious emotion trauma. My time in a "war zone" was brief and uneventful and yet during the three years that bracketed that event was the worst the war had to offer. In the mid 1960's, I was serving a non-medical assignment at one of the largest military hospitals in the Far East.

I watched the daily patient count rise from just over a hundred, most of those being not combat related, to over 700 at the height of the

Tet offensive. I witnessed wounds that were the worse man could inflict on another human being. Our doctors, nurses and corpsmen had to finish to work that began in the field of combat. Repairing severed limbs; doing plastic surgery; rearranging vital organs; performing physical therapy; dealing with both the physical and mental anguishes of war while some of those patients lay waiting in the passageways to be seen or waiting weeks for a bed.

As non-medical personal, we were obliged to perform "duties" of a non-medical nature such as ambulance driver; baggage room and customs (this meant going through a patients personal effects when they finally got around to send them). This that all of their personal belongings were sent to after their arrival. We had boxes filled with weapons; drugs; unauthorized souvenirs (like gold trinkets) and just plain weird crap like human scalps.

We were called upon to perform other duties like human tissue removal from the Operating Rooms. Not pleasant but necessary.

If after the every six hour bed count, someone was missing, we had to secure all the exits and search for the missing patient.

Usually it was uneventful but sometime they were passed out in the head (bathroom) or sleeping in the wrong place or one time, under the hospital. Our hospital was elevated due to close proximity to the ocean. One evening while manning the "After Hours" desk, we had a report that one of our patients from the Psych ward was missing, we secured all the exits and began our search, and my team (per our SOP) had to search one of the four exterior quadrants.

We spotted our patient underneath the hospital about twenty feet in. As the senior ranking team member, it was determined that I needed to go in first to evaluated the situation. With four able-bodied Hospital Corpsman five feet behind, I crawled in and as I got closer, I observed that he was kneeling and looked like he was playing with marbles in his hand. A few long seconds later, he slumped over to the side and we discovered a single edge razor blade in one hand and his testicles in the other. Despite the massive amount of blood loss he survived. If we hadn't found him, he would have become another victim of this war. During the mid-60s through mid-70s, I lost a number of friends; classmates and shipmates in the Vietnam Conflict.

Throughout my life there has been trauma. Motorcycle accidents, numerous surgical procedures to correct motorcycle injuries, dealing with our mother's Alzheimer's, my parents' death, my 5 year old nephew dying while in heart surgery, my best friend's debilitating fall of 50 feet, a bull goring my leg, my daughter losing her leg below the knee, an ex-wife's death, a divorce, and losing a son to suicide when he was 17.

After my son's death in 1982, my therapy involved drinking massive qualities of alcohol. Not only to ease the pain, but to deal with "What could I have done different?" It didn't help. I spent most of his insurance money on things I didn't need; couldn't afford; to impress people I didn't even like. It did however, put me into a different kind a trauma. The trauma of being an alcoholic, just like my father. I never beat anyone; only drank on occasion and never stopped at just one drink. Why? After a few years of sobriety and therapy, it seemed that the trigger for the "binge" was usually related to a significant event or trauma. My deceased son's birthday, anniversaries of his death, any major event were I was expected to attend were some of the triggers. I would go out with a couple of buddies after work, have a few and when they went home to their families; I stayed and had a few more. This caused many encounters with law enforcement.

I've been sober from over 25 years. Still have MANY issues regarding family, anger, health, aging and visions of the past. After many years of packing those traumatic incidents in a box and hiding them in a closet, I've come to realize that is not the best thing for me to do. I know that in the past, counseling has helped, but I still resisted because......I still can't find the answer to that. I try my best to stay busy, but lately health issues has interfered. I want to have patience, but struggle with anger.

I'm a work in progress, and as my mother would often say when there was a crisis, "This stuff only happens to the living."

*First Official PTSD Book Meeting:
Tom Walsh, Ron Papaleoni,
Lynn Hubbard, and Cindy Smith*

PATRIOT GUARD RIDERS

<u>Song by Cindy Smith and T. B. Burton</u>

Just a boy of eighteen years when he left home that day

His mom and dad sent letters to a country far away

After his tour he came home but he was never quite the same

In honor he served his country without regret or shame

He flew the flag in his front yard with unwavering pride

And the sticker on his bumper boldly read Semper Fi.

I could see about a hundred bikes as I recall that day

It must have looked like a parade of flags on the highway

I can still hear their engines roar - echoing in the wind

They're the Patriot Guard Riders - They came

here to escort him.

That morning of the funeral, a day I can't forget

The men who rode from miles away he never even met

They came to show their support for another they had lost

And shield the grieving family from protestors who would cross

They followed in formation to his final resting place

Assuring his arrival there with dignity and grace.

I could see about a hundred bikes as I recall that day

It must have looked like a parade of flags on the highway

I can still hear their engines roar - echoing in the wind

They're the Patriot Guard Riders - They came here to escort him.

They stand for those who stood for us, Firefighters, Military and Police

Those who risk their lives for us, for our freedom, for our peace.

I could see about a hundred bikes as I recall that day

It must have looked like a parade of flags on the highway

I can still hear their engines roar - echoing in the wind

They're the Patriot Guard Riders - They came here to escort him.

MY OWN LITTLE WAR

Kennesaw Taylor

In the nineteen seventies there were two wars raging in my world. Well, that is not exactly true, at our home we were not allowed to watch television or read the news. Viet Nam was only a slight ghost of a thing we only heard whispers of. While this story is not meant to belittle the great tragedies visited upon our countries young men, it is about a much more personal war, my war.

I guess for you to understand my very real connection with PTSD, you would need something to give you a quick introduction to my childhood. Let this article I wrote a couple years ago, stand in evidence of my qualifications.

I Died On Christmas Day

It was December 25, 1968. A god lived in our old house, a god who didn't allow his subjects to come from their room until he emerged from his. Christmas day was no exception and he didn't emerge until after lunch. Four innocent souls stood in doorways trying to get a peek at the tree or the little bundles of heaven wrapped in colored paper and bows.

The day moved on, the egg shells placed carefully to catch unsuspecting little feet were scattered with loving care. Their crunching sounds were barely audible, but screamed in our universe. Step on a crack, break your mothers back, step on a shell go directly to hell.

A mistake was made, by whom, unimportant. The face of our god flushed red, gone was the Christmas god. The remnant of presents were scattered throughout the room, the remnants of breakfast was still on the table, the remnants of a fire smoldered in its place and the remnants of sanity swirled, rose and vanished into the air.

It happened quickly, it always did. I turned to see the fist of god, it has risen and was destined to fall. The first punch took my breath even as I tried to avoid it, a sin in itself. The second busted my lip, the taste of blood its little gift. I knew the taste of blood well. The third to the stomach bent me forward allowing the tooth, already roaming around loose in my mouth to be projected onto the floor at my feet. I concentrated on that unruly tooth as a series of punches came too quick to comprehend and seemingly from all directions at once. The tooth held some importance I could not discern.

My mind raced and screamed into the universe, why, what did I do?

My next gift a broken rib and the sound of a broken nose exploded in my mind. My heart and lungs fought for every moment, but my legs gave up early and I spread across the floor like snow melting in a cozy room. I grasped at consciousness it being all you have.

Now the time of our god's foot had arrived, it kicked, something broke, it kicked, something tore, it kicked and reality shattered then scattered across the floor before my eyes. I could feel death breathing on me as my hair was grasped firmly. My heart pounded in my head or maybe it was my head being pounded on the brick hearth in front of the fireplace. Sickeningly my mind counted the times it rose and fell on the bricks, one, two, ten and twelve, it counted down the seconds of my life. I saw the fire with such clarity, a message from the real God I couldn't comprehend, perhaps? Somewhere in all this, the words, I'll you kill you little son of a so and so, the last words I'd ever hear, wormed their way in. The fear, the pain and the sick, slimy, sticky, warm taste of blood were the memories that came with them. In the end death has a warm, welcoming embrace.

I awakened to find I was mistaken. What do you do the day after you die? What do you do the rest of your life? No police were called, no hospital was visited and no one explained how a dead child is supposed to act. Some things must be figured out by an eight year old, by himself. It only took a couple week of being buried in my room, out of sight of the world, for me to walk this earth again.

Sometimes I am told before, during and after I speak, to GET OVER IT. I have.

I speak because dead children cannot. I speak for children who die at the hands of a monster in a nightmare/horror reality. I speak for the ten children in America, each day, average age three, who are cowering in corners as someone they know love and trust beats them into the silence of death.

I speak because I died several times and God allowed me to come back, he DEMANDS I speak. I speak for the ten children who will die each of the twelve days of Christmas. Every day ten more that live will slip into their own Silent Night and no one will know their names.

I never went to South East Asia, but my war ended at almost the exact same time as the war of so many of my oldest and most admired friends.

I never died to wake up in an army hospital, but I died over a dozen times just the same. I was never shot at, but my step father and tormentor was shot execution style in front of me when I was fourteen. It takes many years to come to terms with the fact that witnessing such a death was the highlight of my life up until that point.

As with many of those who share PTSD, I have never found a friend, family member, spouse or doctor who could hear the truth of what I went through and still look at me the same way again.

There were years of depression which I affectionately called the incredible cloud of doom. In the beginning these episodes were in daily cycles. I might be happy for several days before crashing and being depressed for several more. This cycle repeated itself continuously. After a time these cycles became weekly and later monthly. At some point much later in life they became quarterly and the amount of depressed times shortened as the amount of good times lengthened.

During these cycles I would make bad decisions. I would forsake friends and loved ones. I would quit jobs and begin new careers. It is due to these episodes that I have had almost one hundred jobs in my life.

I suffered through paranoia and even believed myself to be borderline schizophrenia at times. In my days in the military as a young man, fighting became my sport and I excelled at it. Drugs and drinking became my best friends and they were the only things on this earth that comforted me in my misery. I would drink and go out in search of some poor son of a bitch to take out my repressed inadequacies on.

PTSD is born of many things, unimaginable violence starts it, but systematic psychological warfare deepens its grip and firmly sets it into place in the recesses of your mind.

We learn to cope, we soften with the passing of time, but PTSD never goes away. I will always remember the screams of my siblings when we were young. I will never forget the sound of bones breaking or the sound of a bullet hitting flesh. I will never forget the taste of blood.

Mostly, I will never forget all the times I died or the days after each of those near death experiences. I will never understand how a dead eight year old is supposed to act. I have spent my entire life living on borrowed time and feeling terrible guilt for my joy at the death of the only real monster I have ever known.

I have had a good life and have known great love and joy. The paranoia, fear, anger and guilt have subsided, but sometimes late at night when things are good and it gets quiet, I realize that they are still there and they always will be.

THE LAST BREATH

Art by Bernie "Doc" Duff

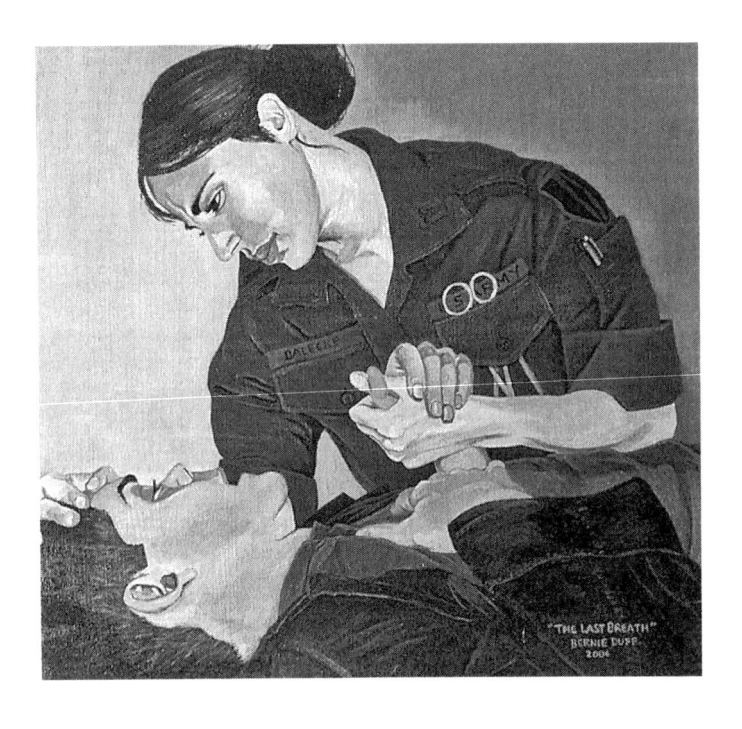

FIRE - FIRE - FIRE - ON THE FLIGHT DECK AFT

Thomas H. Yarmosh

As told to Cindy Smith

I was in the United States Navy, January 29th, 1965 to April 17th, 1968.

It was the USS Forrestal CVA 59. The same ship as John McCain, 2008 Republican Presidential Candidate and United States Senator was on stationed on. The ship was nicknamed, "The USS Forrest Fire" by everyone who knew of it. There were so many fires going on all the time.

I remember the day it happened, the day the ship blew up. The first bomb hit at 10:52 am. Lunch was served between 11:00am and 2:00. I had decided that I was going to skip lunch that day and take a nooner (nap). Just as I jumped on my bunk, I heard the announcement over the P.A. system. *"Fire - Fire - Fire - on the flight deck aft."* There were so many fires on the ship, I figured I am not going to go to another little fire that you could put out with a fire extinguisher.

Then all of a sudden, another explosion knocked me right out of my bunk. I climbed out and up the ladder onto the deck. I had to run back, before I could run forward. (On the left side of the ship - the Port Side - you run back. On the right side - the Star Board - you run forward.) The fire was in the aft, the back third of the ship.

That explosion blew up the P. A. System. No one heard the announcement saying, "All hands forward". Therefore, I ran back. I ran straight into a young kid when I got on deck. He was standing up against the wall - totally white - with an empty stare. It's what they used to call 'shell shock'. I grabbed him, pulled him away from the wall, and told him to run. He didn't move. So, I pushed him through the passage way. Then, a 750 pounder went off behind us. What a noise! The explosion sounded liked a plate glass being shattered throughout the ship. There were quite a few men in front of us. I saw their backs exploding, little holes ripping through their shirts, like matchsticks. Shrapnel.

I kept shoving the kid, and thought, I must be hurt bad myself, but I felt nothing. Later I learned that I only had three holes, just three pieces of shrapnel in my arm, my back and my leg. I eventually pushed the kid into sick bay and I kept going. I went to my General Quarter Station I had just been assigned to. Chief said for me to go anywhere I could help. There were so many injured guys. It was just a whole bunch of craziness.

I worked my way up the flight deck. The planes on the flight deck that day were loaded for bomb runs with who knows what they were dropping that day. The water we were standing in, putting out the fire in the Post Office on board, was orange. Now, I can't say it was Agent Orange that turned the water orange, but it's my best guess that it was. It was coming from the flight deck where the planes were. The government has said, "No Sailor ever came in contact with Agent Orange". But, just how do they think that stuff got over there if it wasn't for the planes on the carriers?

The fire burned for four days before we finally got it under control. I didn't sleep for almost seventy-two hours. There were bodies everywhere. One hundred and thirty-four men were dead. On the fifth day, I ran into a buddy of mine on the ship. He said, 'What are you doing here! You were listed as dead!' I found out that my sister had been calling Washington to see if she could find out any information on me and, thank God, they only had me listed as 'missing'.

When the bomb went off, it was in the Marine Quarters. I would have been there laying in my bunk, but a few days before, I had got into trouble and got a transfer. I had to move to the boat shop down below. My life was spared all because of a little trouble!

I stayed on that ship until it was rebuilt and I was released from duty in 1968. At the time, it was the largest aircraft carrier in the world.

I loved being a civilian again. Me and my best friend, George Cvanciger, decided to take a six month ride across the USA. I met George the day before I left for the Navy. I was taking a ride with my best friend, Augie. The guy in the back seat leaned up front, and put his cigarette out on the skin of my arm. I said, 'Augie, is this guy your friend, 'cause he'd better not do that again, or I'll kill him'. George (the back seat rider) and I have been best friends ever since. All created by a Pall Mall

Cigarette.

The ride was kind of rough coming back home. George and I were driving through Grants, New Mexico, up in the Rockies. We hit some ice on the road and drove off a cliff. We clipped off a few tree tops, rolled over and over a couple of times, and landed seventy-five feet down.

I was trapped, but George managed to climb out. He went looking for help. He found six well-inebriated (American) Indians out there, and they saved our lives. What an adventure that was.

God must have had a better plan for me being here on earth, 'cause I've had many close ones.

Although I was not officially diagnosed with PTSD, I was told by both my parents I had it. When I got home from the service, I could lose my temper in a heartbeat. I don't know why. My second wife always said I had PTSD. I didn't sleep well. I had nightmares. I dreamt I was always being killed - getting shot in the back of the head. Marriage didn't work out for me, but we did have two wonderful children, two sons, Matt and Chris.

I don't understand PTSD. I think

sometimes, maybe it's just the make-up of a person and how they deal with what they've been through. It can happen to you in a heartbeat. Now, the flashbacks - I do understand that.

It could be very easy to become depressed. If you think about things too long, it could drive you crazy. I was really down after my second divorce. I missed tucking my kids into bed every night. I went from seeing them every day to just two days a week. I learned the hard way that you could have the happiest marriage in the world, but that person isn't there to make you happy. You have to make yourself happy.

The PTSD thing - I think it's always gonna be with you. I mean, when you see people die right in front of you, how do you put it behind you?

You have to take your mind away from it. You gotta find something you like to do. And, when you find it, do more of it. That's how I do it.

So, I bought a little farm, rather a little piece of land I'm trying to turn into a farm. It's a work in progress. I just stay busy. I love life and I'm happy. And, George and I are still best friends to this day.

28

OLD MEN WITH BROKEN HEARTS

Song by Charlie May

When I walked in I saw the men, with their backs against wall.
In cowboy hats and combat boots, these old men had seen it all.
 They fought the wars and plowed the fields and worked in factories.
 They did what they had to, to care for their families.

Pete still likes to talk about the year he turned 18.
 Went to work on his dad's farm, and married the girl of his dreams.
 Luke lost his arm in Vietnam in the spring of '65.
 Now he wears a Silver Star and thanks God he's still alive.

Now they're old men with broken hearts, and their backs against the wall,
Still living in the memories, there in the lonely

hall.

They're hoping someone comes today, or maybe they'll just call.
These old men with broken hearts, with their backs against the wall

Sam walks the halls from dust till dawn, and never lifts his head.
There's 12 men on this unit that never leave their bed.
 At night you can hear the cries, as their love ones they call.
 These old men with broken hearts, with their backs against the wall.

Now they're old men with broken hearts, and their backs against the wall,
Still living in the memories, there in the lonely hall.

They're hoping someone comes today, or maybe they'll just call.
These old men with broken hearts, with their backs against the wall.

29

LIFE HASN'T ALWAYS BEEN EASY.

Anonymous

My life hasn't always been easy. It started thirty-seven years ago. For the first eight years of my life, I was abused physically and emotionally and told I was unwanted, a mistake, stupid and the list could go on for miles. My own father beat me over the head with a hammer.

Things finally started changing when I was removed from their care and adopted. I had a family who valued and loved me. By then, I wasn't just a typical teenager. I admit I was a "demon" child. Emotionally, I started acting out everything that had happen to me growing up. I was married for the first time at seventeen, had my first child at eighteen and second at age nineteen. My husband at the time was very angry and violent. It was so bad that at one point, even though I was eight and a half months pregnant, he tried putting his fist through my face.

The marriage lasted five years and then I married again, thinking things had changed. For the most part everything was great; until I found out he cheated on me. I had been so brainwashed by then that I wanted to stay. I felt the only way possible to keep him was to agree to be in the swinging lifestyle. That was that a big mistake, it just gave him "permission" to sleep with whomever he wanted and desensitized me to reality. I was a hollow shell walking around; appearing all was good and happy, when it wasn't.

During this time, I was in the Military. I was involved in a motor vehicle accident that caused me to have a TBI (traumatic brain injury); which in turn caused me to have seizures. Due to my MOS, and non-deployable status, I was allowed to remain in to finish out my contract. Unfortunately, a fellow soldier was out to kill me. By the grace of God, a friend's husband, and fellow brother-in-arms, saved my life.

I finally had the courage to leave my second husband. I decided no more "falling in love" for me. No! I had been through enough already. I retired out of the military and focused on my sons. Eventually, I trusted another man and married again. He truly seemed to care and love me and my sons.

In hind sight, I see he just loved himself and the thought of having a family. He was an alcoholic, which he hid from me the entire time. His addiction was so bad, he went dumpster diving for it. Being married to an alcoholic was draining me and caused me to gain a lot of weight. I went from 135lbs to 220lbs, so unhealthy. With the encouragement from friends and my sons, I finally stepped up and said enough is enough. He either went to an in-house treatment program, or I was done. He chose alcohol over me, no surprise really.

Somewhere along the way, I was diagnosed with PTSD. My PTSD was so bad that nine out of ten times a day I was debating suicide. I had enough abuse and it made me feel worthless. I hid my diagnoses from everyone and put on my happy-go-lucky mask to hide my pain.

In November 2013, I was online talking to friends when I came across a profile that caught my eye. I made a smart ass remark about one of his pictures and we started talking, more teasing one another. Our first date was hiking one of the mountains near our home. Unfortunately, I was so nervous I didn't eat that day. About a quarter of the way into the hike, I literally blacked out. We've been together now almost two years, married one year, three months and ten days, but who's counting, right!

We are both into fitness. I was introduced to a fitness product from very dear friends of ours. I loved it so much that I got him involved with it. It's always better to work out with a partner than alone. I had injured my right ankle and couldn't exercise, but eventually, I was allowed to go back to my daily workouts. I noticed after taking the product for one month, and exercising again, that I had not had any suicidal thoughts or issues with my PTSD. I felt the best I had in years.

I've never taken medication for my PTSD, I refused. I knew it would cause me to be that "walking shell" again. I attribute my surviving with my PTSD to God, my husband and Shakeology, the fitness product we used. Please understand that I do not know if this product, or exercise program, will help everyone the way it has me, but if it helps one more person, it's worth stepping out of my comfort zone and sharing my story.

HOOAH

ANOTHER PTSD NIGHT

Poem by Kerry "Doc" Pardue

Another night of little sleep
One of endless nights of little sleep
Such is my life
Night, after night, after night
I dream about another place another time
Of taking lives
And losing others
The sounds, the voices, the images so real;
Then I realize that they aren't happening now
Wish I could leave them in the past
Almost asleep now
Did you see that????
A rat the size of a cat!!!

31

THE MANY FACES OF PTSD

George Woodruff

PTSD has a long history. It has been known by many different names in many different wars and is as old as mankind. I first made its acquaintance, in 1945, as an eighteen year old sailor who was a patient in Oakland Naval Hospital with a temporal lobe seizure disorder from a brain injury that had been diagnosed as anxiety. Back during World War Two PTSD was called combat or battle fatigue or combat exhaustion. The open psychiatric ward where I resided contained about two dozen men in "side by side" beds. Most were either combat marines or naval personnel who were veterans of bloody South Pacific battles where casualty rates were almost beyond belief. They had been through a living hell and it had left them with memories and emotional problems they could not shake. Memories of landing craft being blown out of the water as they attempted to land...buddies shot to pieces right next to them...the slog across the small islands against an entrenched enemy determined to kill them...the screams of wounded and dying men calling out to God or their mothers for help that never came.

I remember the small Marine in the bed next to me. At night I could hear his sobs as he lay there awake and sleepless. He had been in the battle of Tarawa, in November, 1943, and had made the landing on Betio...Tarawa's largest island. Both the landing and the seventy six hour battle were bloody with over 1000 marines killed and more than 2000 wounded. Although he went on to fight in other South Pacific battles...try as he might...he could not shake the image of Betio from his thoughts. Finally he ended up in Oakland Naval Hospital diagnosed with combat fatigue. He was constantly angry and irritable...carrying memories of horror he could not forget. It left an impression on me and I will remember it and him as long as I live. The war ended while we were patients and both of us were medically discharged shortly after Japan's surrender. I often wonder how it affected his ability to adjust to civilian life as the load he was carrying was almost too much for any man. Did he eventually adjust or did he end it all because he could not live with the pain? I certainly hope it was the former.

My next meeting with what I later discovered to be PTSD took place in a psychiatric ward in Crile VA Hospital, in Cleveland, Ohio, in 1946. It was encased in the form of a young Army veteran of Italian extraction we called "Specks". Specks had served in the European theatre going across France into Belgium and finally into Germany. He had seen plenty of death and dying and it had left an indelible mark upon him. He was labeled as having "combat fatigue". What were his visible symptoms? He had difficulty falling asleep and when he did he would wake up sobbing and whimpering. He would have outbursts of anger for no discernible reason and if you came up on him from behind it was like he was going to jump out of his skin. He avoided contact with most of the other patients and if they persisted in bothering him he would explode. For some reason he and I got along well and we could share our experiences. I liked him. He was Italian and his mother would often bring him delicious Sicilian pizza which he would share with me. When I was discharged he was still there. I never saw him again.

After my discharge from the Navy, I drank heavily and could not settle down. I roamed the United States...hitchhiking from shore to shore. I often spent the night in local jails, shelters, and even out in the open. In 1947, I joined the Army. Although I did not realize or understand it, I still had my undiagnosed temporal lobe seizure problem due to a fall in the Navy. I simply ignored it. Things went along fairly well until I was sent to serve in Germany during the Berlin Airlift. I was eventually hospitalized in Army hospitals and every now and then I would meet patients who suffered from what is now called PTSD. Their symptoms would be much the same as those I had witnessed in the Marine I slept next to in the Oakland Naval Hospital and my friend, Specks, at Crile Veterans Hospital. Once you have been a patient in a military or VA psychiatric ward and seen someone suffering with combat fatigue, PTSD, or whatever name it goes under at the time you will recognize it immediately. It is unforgettable!

My next meeting with PTSD took place in Germany when I was hospitalized again in a psychiatric ward in Frankfurt's 97th General Army Hospital. About half the patients there were regular Army combat veterans who would have met the criteria for a PTSD diagnosis.

I began to realize that the condition was widespread. It was still diagnosed as combat fatigue and one of the treatments used was something called electroshock therapy. It was kind of primitive at the time. You were lined up in the hall waiting to go into a small room that held a cot and a psychiatrist with some kind of shock machine. They would place electrodes bilaterally on your temples, a rubber piece in your mouth, and "bam" you would wake up walking down the hall hurting all over and trying to remember where you were.

I had six of those shock treatments myself and I can attest to the fact that as crude as they were in 1949 they actually did some good. At least you lost a lot of your memories...some good ones and some bad ones. I came back from Germany, on the USS Comfort, in late 1949. I was first hospitalized in Walter Reed where I saw more cases of what we now call PTSD. In early 1950 I was transferred to the Army's Brooke General Hospital, in San Antonio, Texas, and was discharged a few months after the Korean War began...again diagnosed with anxiety.

As my condition worsened I spent a lot of time in and out of VA Hospital psychiatric wards where a full fifty percent of the veterans there would meet the requirements for a PTSD diagnosis. I began to realize that this was a condition that required treatment and it was not being given. Most of the veterans (me included) were given electroshock therapy. In the early 1960's I received an additional fifteen treatments bringing my total up to twenty one. Large chunks of my memory disappeared and still haven't returned after sixty years. I did become more placid and, although the seizures continued, I still had a lot of psychological damage which I carry to this day.

In 1974 my trips to VA psychiatric wards ceased and were exchanged for trips to VA neurological wards instead. The VA finally recognized that I was an epileptic and began to give me seizure medications instead of tranquilizers. My seizures continued and worsened from overdoses my system could not handle. From then on seeing fellow patients who I could recognize as having PTSD was rare. It became obvious that this was a specific condition and in 1980 the American Psychiatric Association finally codified "post-traumatic stress disorder" in the Statistical Manual of Mental Disorders. As for me…in 1981 after many EEG's and three weeks in Gainesville VA Hospital a medication was found that stopped my seizures. I still have the neurologist's medical report as it pointed out that the original diagnosis was incorrect. Although the epilepsy was finally under control the problems that went with it remained.

The final case of PTSD I have inadvertently witnessed is my own. While I could recognize its effects on me I never realized I had it and denial of the facts was my escape from the truth. It obviously came from my experiences in the military and it remains with me until this very day. It is hard to live with, hard to understand, and even harder on the ones who love you when it exhibits itself. I am better controlled than I was during my military service in the Army and Navy and during my many hospitalizations in VA psychiatric wards over the years. Having gone down the same road as others myself, I can understand what those who suffer with PTSD are going through and how extremely disabling it can be. I can also understand those suicidal thoughts that run through the mind of some who live with it day after day. Acceptance is better today now that PTSD is recognized and has lost the stigma that was formerly attached to it when many people believed that it was weakness of character, a mental disorder; you were just plain nuts!

PTSD is by no means always a single disease. It often manifests itself in association with features such as depression and anxiety. While I had a type of epilepsy from a fall from the top of a three decker bunk to a concrete floor in the Navy that knocked me unconscious, and is the obvious cause of my unusual seizure disorder, medicine had not progressed far enough at that time to diagnose it correctly. I think the same problem may have occurred with what we now identify as PTSD and as a result it was treated as a totally different psychiatric problem. The electroshock treatments which were given early on apparently helped somewhat in certain cases by erasing memories. PTSD is a disabling disease that affects fully a third of combat veteran to one extent or another. Continued research is required to find better ways of treating it. While we know the cause of PTSD, the solution that will provide necessary relief or an eventual cure may still be far away. Unfortunately it is part of the terrible cost of war and those who suffer from it cannot be ignored.

THOSE WHO CAME HOME...

Dwane Barr

Out in the desert, somewhere alone,
Mike and his partner made,
A dune base their home.
The climate was dry, dry as a bone.

With no comforts, not even a fire,
Conditions were desperate and yes, even dire.
Their mission was dangerous,
They fought for all of us.

To make people free and safe from enemies,
Soldiers gave up their lives and sanities.
They volunteered to save the Earth,
From every scourge, they showed their worth.

Shots sounded far away,
Maybe they would not fight today.
Resting in the sand,
No one to give a hand.

Isolation for days at a time,

PTSD-NO APOLOGIES

Always careful to watch for mines.
They moved to rejoin their team
Getting closer it seemed.

At last to see our flag,
Their burdens fell like a worn out rag.
Fell upon their knees to thank
The beautiful red, white, and blue.

Safe at last to give a mighty thanks,
To Him that that rejoined their ranks.
The war goes on, no rest for our soldiers,
Some come home and others stay over.

War is hard on a man,
Even when they return.
Women too, often got burned,
What is the lesson, what have we learned?

Can we heal all those who were injured?
Will we restore their broken minds?
Can we reward those who gave so much?
The answer I think lies in us.

MY JOURNEY HOME

Zach Choate

As told to Cindy Smith

I served in the United States Army, January 2005 to June 2008. I was deployed to Iraq in August 2006, 10th Mountain Division; Fort Drum, New York.

In October of 2006, I was the Gunner for the platoon leader when we were hit by a road side bomb.

According to Iraqi law, citizens are only allowed to have one weapon per household and only a certain amount of ammunition. In one home, we located and found several AK-47's. My unit confiscated the AK-47's. Because the paperwork to log in the weapons is such a pain, we decided go the "black route". That is to say, we dumped them into the canal. The road to the canal was notorious for having mines and road side bombs, but it was the only route to get there in order to dispose of the guns. We were fresh into deployment, just six months. As the gunner, I sat above the truck and had a camera, taking shots of the area looking for possible hiding spots. Standing up on the gunner strap and surveying the area, I observed a military age male driving back and forth on a tractor. It was farm land, but still he looked suspicious. Odd. We dumped the AK's into the canal, got back in the truck, and started to roll.

That's when the road bomb went off. It must have been cell phone activated. It was a huge charge, meant to destroy something bigger, like taking out a tank. Because of the magnitude of the bomb, it sent the truck flying in the air about thirty feet. There was a massive cloud of smoke. I was ejected from the gunner's turret. Among the injuries I suffered, I had a punctured lung, fractured ribs, traumatic brain injury and a lacerated spleen.

Five months later, I volunteered to return to my unit as a Calvary Scout, inside Baghdad's 'Triangle of Death'. I served there until my deployment ended in November 2007.

I was awarded the Purple Heart for my service, The Order of Maurice Infantry Award, and other various medals.

When I came home, there was a wedge

between me and my family. I thought they were different, changed. It took me awhile before I realized that it was me that had changed, not them.

I remember they used to say, 'Why can't you just snap back into reality?' It would really get under my skin. They didn't know what to do with me. They didn't know what I was going through. They weren't there. I was hurting and my reality was scarred, transformed by my experiences. I was not the same.

The VA officially diagnosed me with PTSD in 2008. I filed a claim and waited more than a year to get my records back from the military. I waited seven more months for my disability claim to go through. I struggled with the VA, jumping through their hoops and hurdles at every turn.

Everything with the VA starts and ends with medication. Some of the Veteran suicides you hear about could be the result of all the lethal amount of pills they give you. They put you on so many anti-depressants, five or six different ones, and the side effects just trickle down. Not to mention it encourages addiction. And, the pills only suppress your emotions and problems, they don't fix anything.

PTSD restricts everything, every portion of your life. It's a daily struggle. I've become aware of my triggers. I stay busy. I stay plugged into people and stay as far away from isolation as possible. I don't necessary like it, *(being around people)* but I need it - to be well. It helps them understand me better, observe and witness what I'm like. You can't expect people to understand you if they're not around you.

I have the nightmares. Sometimes my dreams are a combination of then and now. I can't separate them, it's weird. It's like I could be in full combat gear, but I'm here and running through a parking lot or something. In another dream, I am sniped out, shot in the head. I can see it. I can feel what it's like to be shot, although I have no idea what a shot in the head feels like.

I'm hyper vigilant, restless, and I'm easy to anger. And, the flashbacks - I get lost inside my head. I'm told I get quiet when it happens. It takes a while to come back, but something snaps, and then I say, 'It's OK, I'm here'.

Then, there's the guilt. The guilt of what I've done over there to 'some' innocent people, *(not all of them were innocent)* and of not being able to be part of the effort anymore, to serve. The guilt that I could have done more, I should have done more, but I wish I didn't have to do any of it.

There is no way to combat PTSD; you just have to find a way to live with it. The things I've experienced over there will stay with me forever. I've spent the last few years looking for ways to heal. It has only been through trial and error along the way that I've learned what I needed to do.

In the past, my name and story has been used by different organizations for their own causes, my words taken out of context, and used to deliver their own personal messages. I didn't see that at the time.

In Savannah, Georgia, at an art studio, I took part in a project to transform Army uniforms into something new and positive. We took a razor and shredded uniforms into scraps, and pounded the pieces until they were nothing but paste. The paste turned into paper and the paper into art. I was tired of taking the pills, tired of the drama that followed me home, and trying to find a way to cope with my life. I'm not anti-war, not anti-military; this was just me, trying to fix me.

I started speaking out on the 'cost of war.'

October 28, 2008 was the first day of my speaking tour where I testified, told my story of what was going on over there. The Government was spending 720 million dollars a day for the war in Iraq, and nobody really knew where it was going.

I participated in peace activities, one being in front of the White House on December 16, 2010. It was organized by the group, 'Veterans for Peace', in opposition to the wars in Afghanistan and Iraq. I've spoke at the same rallies as Daniel Ellsberg and Ralph Nader. I worked with the 'Wounded Warriors', and I like what they have to say - 'You are not alone'. It sounds good when you say it, and in one way it's OK. But, especially in small town, that's not how it is. Vets are hiding. We don't know how to handle life outside of the military. I think Vets need Vets to talk with, there's that brotherhood, that connection.

There's a big disassociation between Veterans and civilians. You don't know what to say, what to do. People may extend their hand and thank a Vet for his service, and our freedom. They put a yellow ribbon on their car antennas, or plaster on bumper stickers that say they support our troops. A lot of people think it stops there. It doesn't. It's not their fault. We need more communication and understanding to close the gap.

I got a dog in 2006. Her name is Burgundy. She's not a registered PTSD dog, but she does recognize and know my triggers, even when I'm sleeping. I got tattoos - statements to myself. Visual reminders of my journey home.

In March 2014, I quit drinking, got sober, and stopped taking my anti-depressants. I'm now a farmer. Nobody gets hurt farming. I like that. I actually read somewhere that farming is the number one ideal occupation for returning vets with PTSD.

On Memorial Day, I planted 22 American flags alongside a road in my hometown. The 22 flags represent the number of Veterans that commit suicide every day. I laid out an additional 1050 more flags, in remembrance. If just one person drives by and looks at them, and it makes them think about the meaning behind it, then it's worth it.

I keep trying different things like this, in hope for more awareness from the public and a little bit more closure for me.

And, the Iraqi war and freedom thing, I don't buy into that. What we're doing over there in Iraq is not for America's freedom. Yes, our 'fear of losing our freedom' maybe. But, it's obliviously about something else. At the end of the day, what I did, I did it for the guys on my left and on my right. We did it for each other.

EVERY DAY IS MEMORIAL DAY

Poem by Kerry "Doc" Pardue

Every Day is Memorial Day

Today we remember

A grateful Nation recalls

Our Men and Women

Who paid the price

Of freedom for us all

For those of us who

Served beside them

Every day is Memorial Day

We can't let their memories fade

We were touched by their loss

Their lives touched ours

Changing and helping us

Becoming who we are

Grateful for what we have

Freedom at Home

For those left at home

You gave us your sons and daughters

Husbands and Wives

Fathers and Mothers

Brothers and Sisters

Friends and Lovers

Thank you for sharing them with us

We miss them all

We won't let them be forgot

That is why each of us

Who have been in battle knows

We can never ever forget

That Every Day is Memorial Day

35

THE LONG DARK ROAD

Jim Elliott

Almost everyone I know that joined the military, joined with an overwhelming sense of strength and pride. We went into the military feeling a little scared and doubtful of what we would do and what we would become. But, ultimately we felt conviction and patriotism. Basic training in the Army only served to bolster all those feelings for me and on graduation day I remember feeling invincible. As the soldiers from my basic training unit stood at attention, we became statues of strength, determination and sheer will. Not an eye blinked, not a muscle twitched and not a breath escaped my mouth too loudly. As our Commander spoke of the obstacles we had overcome and of our accomplishments, we felt like soldiers. We gave no thoughts to our future, of the things to come, we were in the here and now and we reveled in it.

Making your way in military life is easy, you just follow everyone else. You want to find the chow hall, you just follow the crowd. You want to be the best, you just find the best and they will teach you. If you want to improve your run, you run with the fast group. Military life is in fact very easy for the most part but there are certain things you never discuss and you learn that early on.

You can talk about your PT or physical training score, your rifle marksmanship score, your NCO evaluation, etc. There is one thing that is never ever talked about and that is your mental status. You can talk about diarrhea, you can talk about cramps or even sex openly, but if you're depressed, anxious or anything remotely like that, it's off limits. I've heard many people say it's just the warrior or military culture to not admit weakness and I feel this is the farthest thing from the truth. If you have ever served you will know it's whole heartedly military to talk about deficiencies; in fact it's why we do so much training. If you're deficient in your shooting skills you will go to the range whenever you can until your scores are satisfactory. If you have low physical training scores you will be made to do remedial physical training until your scores are high. If you're going to PLDC, or primary leadership school, to become a Non Commissioned Officer and you can't find your way to the chow hall, you will do land navigation till you hate it but it will be second nature.

The problem is that as soldiers, we were trained to deal with physical situations and to reaction to those situations. Were taught how to deal with suffering in all types of environments and war. Even our courses are designed that way. Reaction to chemical weapons, reaction to small arms fire, and reaction to mortar attack. Every single one of these has the same thing in common; it's how we react to a physical problem. We are very well versed in the seen, problems that we can solve with a physical reaction. The problem is that we are given almost no training on how to react to the unseen. We are told if a fellow soldier is withdrawn or is acting funny to alert your chain of command. The problem is if you alert your chain of command about this then you will be an outcast and shunned by fellow soldiers, even called a "Blue Falcon" or buddy fucker. You can talk to your fellow soldiers but they rarely, if ever, will tell you if something is wrong, I know because I didn't.

I started having issues in my second year of service. My hands would shake uncontrollably; I would get chills and night sweats and have violent thoughts. I did not have PTSD or anything associated with being in a war time situation but for some reason I would get overly anxious. Finally in 2001, I had an incident in the chow hall. My hands were shaking so violently that I could not hold my tray steady. I could not think and my heart began racing. I tried to leave, but there was a line of soldiers in the way and I became physically violent. I remember feeling a sense of impending doom and screaming I was "going to die". I was tackled to the ground by the mess sergeant and several other soldiers. I remember bits and pieces of the military police rushing in, holding me down and handcuffing me as I struggled to get free. I was put on a gurney and shackled as they rushed me out to the ambulance, still fighting. I remember them saying I was on drugs or something like that and slivers of being given a shot once I got to Eisenhower Medical Center, then blackness.

I woke up to my Platoon Sergeant and a Military Police Officer in my room; I felt drugged and couldn't open my eyes. My Platoon Sergeant came to my bedside and said, "Hey El, how are you doing?" My mouth was so dry I couldn't speak and for a moment I had no idea where I was. The first thing my Sergeant asked me was how I was feeling. I responded that I was ok but I felt loopy. The MP told me that I had an outburst in the chow hall and had to be sedated. They said I needed to speak up about the drugs I was taking and I might get off with counseling and restriction to base. I told them repeatedly I had not taken any drugs and then I was treated like a prisoner. My Platoon

Sergeant was told to leave under protest and then two CID officers came to see me later that day. I was told that I injured four soldiers and that when the blood tests came back and I was "hot", they would court martial me for not coming forward. I explained I didn't do drugs but they pressured me to sign a statement and tell them where I got the drugs. I refused to sign a statement and eventually the blood tests came back negative.

I was remanded to my barracks and shortly after I left the hospital under supervision, I was ordered to mental health. No one would talk to me or look me in the eye and I couldn't go anywhere on my own. I was taken to my appointment by my section Sergeant and it was quiet the whole way. Keep in mind, up to this point I was a model soldier. I was a team player; this was my second duty station. I had went TDY, or temporary duty, on many assignments and won several awards. I was fast tracked to being a Specialist, or E-4, in only a little over 2 years and I had never had any real problems, but now I was a leper. It was first determined I had an anxiety disorder and I had to take classes and medications to control it. Then I was told it was depression with anxiety and given more pills. I was never asked about it by my chain of command and I never brought it up to anyone. About three months after the incident, things got back to normal and it seemed all was forgotten. I want to say this, I had an amazing chain of command and I respected them all. There just was no SOP, or standard operating procedure, for this, so if it was not talked about then it just went away.

As my military career progressed, I became an acting section Sergeant and eventually I received my Corporal rank. I had been through airborne school, Air assault school and reclassed so that I had two military job classifications and I quit taking my pills. Everything was fine, or so it seemed, and even when it was not I never said a word. One of the things that kept me grounded was my marriage in late 2002. I always had slight issues which I kept under control but having a wife and child to take care of seemed to keep the demons at bay. Deployment or some long, late night guard duties, were when the demons in my head seemed to really show their ugly face. Often it was all I could do to make it through the night. No matter how bad it got, I still never said a word.

In 2003, I was injured badly in a falling accident and had to have major back surgery. The stress of this seemed to make everything in my head so loud I could not think. After my surgery, it was determined that for my continued health, I was no longer able to carry a ruck sack on my back. Since any MOS, or military occupational specialty in the U.S. Army, required that I wear a ruck sack, I was given a military discharge. I fought hard to stay, to reclass or anything that would keep me in the Army. I had reference letters from my chain of command, my command Sergeant Major and even from a one star General that I drove for. But, by the powers that be determined, I was unfit for duty. So I was given a medical discharge, a severance package of $30,000 dollars and a service connection of

30% for a broken back and a lifetime of pain.

After my discharge, I began to sink into depression and sought the help of the V.A. since I had no medical insurance. I was put back on the same medications I was on in the military and seemed to get better for a time. I really was never asked much as far as how I was feeling, the V.A. just mirrored everything the Army did and then after a while that didn't help. I started doing more and more self-destructive things until it was too much for my family to bear. I fought, had bad temper outbursts and I had many affairs. This is not to say all of this was due to mental health. My marriage was falling apart and some of this was a bi-product of that. I was terrible to live with and often became angry at the tiniest transgressions. Then I started hearing and seeing things. In the Army, I sometimes heard things or even saw things but it was a rare occurrence and I shook it away. I talked to my mental health doctor in the Army and was told it was just stress induced psychosis. I was told that it was my body's way of dealing with all the stress and my anxiety. Now it was becoming a big problem and I didn't know what to do.

On the morning of April 3rd, 2006, I was sitting in my living room with a Glock 19 in my hand. I had loaded a few rounds in the magazine and it was in my hand resting in my lap. The voices had grown so loud and violent I didn't know what to do and I felt I had no choice but to end it all. As I was looking at the weapon in my hand, my son who was only around seven at the time, came into the living room. He said he was thirsty and wanted a glass of water. So I got him a glass of water and put him to bed. After this, I drove to the VA; saw my doctor and he was very condescending. I was told that veterans just wanted a hand out and that we were trying to get over on the system. This was at the V.A. medical center in Dayton Ohio. I flew off the handle; I lifted the doctor's desk and turned it over. He ran from the room screaming and I went after him. He locked himself in the administration room and a half second later, I was being beaten and tasered by the V.A. police. I was shackled and given Thorazine and they immediately put me on suicide watch, lock down. I was there for a week.

At this point I was rediagnosed as having Bi polar, Schizophrenia. My mental health Doctor believed I had been misdiagnosed from the start and that the anxiety and depression medications actually made the issue worse. So I was put on anti-psychotic medications, but the V.A. or my doctor, ever apologize and now I had the label of "Violent" stamped across my mental health file.

The first medications I was put on made me jumpy and irritable, the second made me even more so. I felt like nothing would help and I tried to keep it tucked away inside. Finally I started feeling better on a mix of lithium and Geodon. I could finally breath and the voices and visions seemed to fade into the background. It had taken six years since I left the army for me to feel good again, but it did happen. I was still having problems in my marriage due to some rather fresh wounds and serious indiscretions on my part, although things were looking up. Problem is, like a lot of people who take mental health medications, I started feeling better and in December, 2010, and I stopped taking them.

On New Year's Eve 2010, I ended up having to work since it was a government contract at Wright Patterson Air Force Base. It would be a quick night so I figured I would come home and watch the ball drop with my wife and kids. I got to work and started feeling anxious. The lights were burning my eyes and my hands began shaking half way through the night. My buddy who was working with me that night kept asking me if I was ok. I don't know if he saw the physical signs that I was having mental issues or he just felt it but somehow he knew. I just explained I was not feeling well and we continued our work. My buddy had plans to meet some people after work for New Year Eve, and so we hurried. The quicker we got done, the quicker we both got to go home. We finished up, and then had the Government employees let us out to go home. I remember it was bitterly cold with about 4 feet of snow on the ground and I actually liked that feeling of the cold enwrapping you as you walk out of a warm building.

On the drive home, I felt as if there was something wrong and my heart was beating a mile a second. I pulled into the driveway and went inside. All the kids were asleep and my wife and a friend were watching the rocking New Year's Christmas special on TV. I went inside and kissed my wife and said happy New Year. I felt exhausted and the light hurt my eyes so I decided just to go to bed. As I was lying in bed, I couldn't sleep and the voices in my head were growing louder along with what seemed like the worst headache I had ever had. I decided to smoke a cigarette and realized that I had left my cigarettes on the counter in the kitchen. I put on my slippers and robe, since one of my female friends was in the house. I got up and went down the hall to the living room. I will not recount what happened next, it is extremely personal and what I think finally sent me over the edge. I left the home, and drove around aimlessly. I had no concept of space or time only that my mind was telling me to do very bad things. I finally called a friend.

I think this point is where I tell you I couldn't get any lower. I did not care about life at this point and I was unsure of what to do next. All I can tell you is that I thank God every day that I just happened to call the right friend at the right time and I am alive today because of it. I had carried all this around without ever really talking about it and finally I let go like I was releasing a flood. My friend talked me into going to the VA and trying to get help. I didn't want to go because of how I had been treated in the past but I decided to do it not for myself but for my children.

Before I go any further, I want anyone reading this to understand this is not a review of the VA in and of itself. I know a lot of amazing, caring people that work for the VA. This next part is a scathing review of how the VA police are trained to deal with veterans with mental health issues. I am writing this because of what happened next and hope this never happens to anyone else.

I am now sitting in my truck outside the VA

medical center in Dayton, Ohio. I just hung up the phone with a friend and decided to go inside the VA to seek help. I slowly walk through the ice and snow, desperate to not feel the way I am feeling. My legs are heavy and my mind is racing. I feel like tiny daggers are stinging my eyes from the inside and all I want is to feel numb.

I walk through the double doors and to the back of the hallway where a nurse's station is with a sign in sheet. There is no pen and I just crumple against the wall to the nurse's office. Several minutes later a nurse comes out and asks me if I'm ok, she tells me that she guesses I am next since I am the only one in the waiting room. I try to get up and she helps me by taking hold of my arm. As she slowly walks me into the nurses' station, she begins to ask me what is wrong. I remember answering the general questions, I tell her what happened and how I'm feeling. I tell her I'm not currently on medications and I lie about wanting to hurt myself. I tell her all I want is to talk to my doctor on the phone, that's all I need to do. At this point, all I can think of doing is talking to my doctor and trying to come to some kind of conclusion, because in my mind maybe he will have some sort of answer for me. The nurse walks me to the back and slides her ID to take me into the emergency room.

I then get placed in a room with a camera and an open door for what seems like an eternity. I feel alone and my heart is racing. Then the nurse comes to the door and all I remember saying is, "I just want to speak to my doctor". The nurse left then came back a few more times. I repeated the same thing every time, "I just want to speak to my doctor!" This last time was much more insistent. Finally the nurse comes in and tells me that they have spoken to my doctor and that I have to put on a pair of medical pajamas if I want to talk to him. I told her that I would not put on the pajamas until I've spoken with him since I didn't intend to stay. She went out and got another nurse that told me the same thing and once again I refused. Shortly after, the main nurse I was dealing with came in and handed me some meds, she said they would relax me and I decided to take them and she left. I remember looking at the clock, it read 3:30am, and then feeling dizzy and looking back at the clock and it was 4:02am.

I remember feeling my legs go numb and I decided to stand but it was very difficult. Then before I knew it, there were several VA police officers standing at my door. The officer in front was much larger than the rest and was in full tactical gear from head to toe. He walked towards me holding the pajamas and telling me I was going to put them on or "he was going to make me!" I felt unsteady and confused and he began to get closer and even more aggressive. I remember feeling rage and telling him that I only wanted to speak to my doctor. He just laughed at me and said, "I guess it's going to be the hard way!" I felt him shove me hard against a wall and I struck him back, he was wrestling me and he felt strong, but I was determined and I twisted him to the side so that he fell over the medical bed. I could not think clearly and my legs were weak, but I tried to run through the other men and knocked one backwards. Another two men grabbed me and sprayed something in my eyes, it burned like fire and I knew it was pepper spray. I grabbed the guy holding my right arm and threw him into the direction I was being sprayed from. From behind me, I felt something strike my head and then electricity enter through my chest. I was on my knees and again I felt something hit my back and the sharp sting of electricity as I fell flat on the floor and then nothingness.

I woke several moments later with my hands and feet tied behind my back. There was a nurse wiping my eyes with chemical wipes but my eyes were swollen closed. I vomited again and again and it felt like I was breathing in the flames from a blow torch. I heard the nurse scream, "was all this really necessary!"

After I was cleaned up and they helped me put on my pajamas, I was taken to the mental health holding unit. I was told to shower while a VA police officer and a nurse stood there. I was then given a shot and put in a bed at which point I passed out. The next day I awoke with a bandage on the back of my head and handcuffed to my bed with burns on my chest and back. I screamed for several minutes and a nurse came into the room with a VA police officer who unhandcuffed me and they took me out to have breakfast. I was there for four days and didn't talk to anyone or see anyone. On the fifth day, my doctor came and got me and took me to a private office down the hall from my room.

I began to ask my doctor why this happened to me and that all I wanted to do was talk to him. He told me the report said I attacked the VA police without provocation and that I was violent from the moment I got to the emergency room, even saying I wanted to harm myself. There was no mention of me being tased or attacked by four to five VA police, even though I still had the burns. There was no mention of them hitting me in the back of the head, even though you could see the dried blood and they bandaged me.

At the end of the day, my doctor did believe

my story and an investigation was launched. One of the nurses who took care of me that night even wrote a statement saying I was acting erratic but not violent or confrontational, and she felt the force used against me was excessive. I spent all together three weeks in the mental health ward and resumed my medications.

I feel this story is important to get out for several reasons. The first is that VA Police are not taught how to deal with veterans with mental health disorders. It does not matter whether you have PTSD, schizophrenia, depression or any other mental illness, you should not be treated this way. This is a story of a bad reaction to something that could have been easily solved. The VA reacted badly, and even worse, they tried to cover it up. I have had many, many good interactions with the VA and most of the time they know exactly what to do, but these bad reactions are the reason that so many veterans refuse to seek help and why so many avoidable tragedies take place.

I urge every veteran to continue to seek

help with the VA or outside service provider if they have the means. I am writing this not to dissuade veterans but to encourage them to use the VA and help change the system. It is easy to forget that if you have a mental illness you are literally one medication dose away from lapsing back into depression or anxiety. Sometimes, when you're feeling good, it's easy to say I don't need these pills anymore. Anyone with mental illness must stay vigilant. You would not go into combat without your weapon and when you have mental illness you cannot combat life without your medications. Please reach out if you need help and do everything you can to keep your mind healthy.

36

YOUR STORY

SPONSORS

American Legion Post 304
www.post304.org

Beach Body Coach
www.beachbodycoach.com/islandtime1106

Cowboy World Atlanta
www.cowboyworldatlanta.com

Lemon Press Publishing
www.lemonpresspublishing.com

Patriot Guard Riders of GA
www.pgrofga.com

200

CONTRIBUTORS INFORMATION:

Cindy Smith
www.cowboyworldatlanta.com
txredmollie@yahoo.com

Jon Broderick
Jon.broderick55@gmail.com

Kennesaw Taylor
kennesaw@kennesawtaylor.com
www.kennesawtaylor.com

Kerry Pardue
www.kerrypardue247.com

Lynn Hubbard
www.lynnhubbard.com
authorlynnhubbard@gmail.com

All Contributors can be contacted at:
lemonpresspublishing@gmail.com

or

Lemon Press Publishing
PO Box 459
Emerson, GA 30137

Index

Anonymous, 16, 43, 138
Bartholomew Gray, 69
Bernie "Doc" Duff, 128
Charlie May, 24, 50, 136
Chris deRoux, 109
Cindy Smith, xv, 10, 43, 60, 70, 105, 117, 129, 155
David Silfer, 70
Dwane Barr, 8, 153
George Woodruff, 143
Gerald "Dino" McGrath, 10
Hugh Lee Young, 60
James (Jim) Filhart, 105
Jim Elliott, 165
John Fredericks, 81
Jon Broderick, 29
Kennesaw Taylor, 120
Kerry "Doc" Pardue, 15, 39, 142, 163
Lynn Hubbard, iii, xi, xxi, 13, 28, 58
Paden Smith, 78
Ranger Bill, 1, 7
Rebecca Fredricks, 102
Ron Asby, 53
Ron Papaleoni, 110
T. B. Burton, 117
Thomas H. Yarmosh, 129
Zach Choate, 155

Also from Lemon Press:
Just Before Taps